Every Day We Will Bless You

I will extol you, my God and King,
   and bless your name forever and ever.
Every day I will bless you,
   and praise your name forever and ever.
                  Psalm 145:1-2

Every Day We Will Bless You

A Book of Daily Prayer

Katherine Kinnamon

Michael Kinnamon

CBP Press

St. Louis, Missouri

All scripture quotations are from the *New Revised Standard
Version of the Bible*, copyright © 1990 by the Division of Christian
Education of the National Council of Churches of Christ in the
United States of America and are used by permission.

Library of Congress Cataloging-in-Publication Data
Kinnamon, Michael
    Every day we will bless You: a book of daily prayer / by
Michael Kinnamon and Katherine Kinnamon.
    ISBN 0-8272-0807-3
    1. Prayer-books.   I. Kinnamon, Katherine.   II. Title
BV245.K546   1990
242' .2—dc20

Contents

Acknowledgments and Dedication

This book was conceived and begun during the summer of 1987, which we spent at the United Theological College (UTC) in Bangalore, India. We wish to express appreciation to our employers (at that time)—the Christian Theological Seminary (Indianapolis) and the regional office of the Christian Church (Disciples of Christ) in Indiana—for allowing us the opportunity to teach, study, and write in India. We also want to thank the Division of Overseas Ministries of the Christian Church (Disciples of Christ) for its financial contribution to our time abroad. Finally, appreciation goes to our new friends at UTC where we found an excellent environment for pursuing this project.

During our time in India, we learned that our good friend, the Reverend Joyce Montgomery Foulkes, had finally succumbed to the cancer that had weakened her body, though not her spirit, for nearly ten years. Joyce knew the meaning and importance of daily prayer; she taught many of us a great deal about what it means to trust daily in the mercy of God. We dedicate this book to her memory and her ministry.

K.K.
M.K.

"In the morning, while it was still very dark, he got up and went out to a deserted place, and there he prayed" (Mark 1:35).

"Hear, O Israel: The LORD is our God, the LORD alone. You shall love the LORD your God with all your heart, and with all your soul, and with all your might. Keep these words that I am commanding you today in your heart. Recite them to your children and talk about them when you are at home and when you are away, when you lie down and when you rise" (Deuteronomy 6:4-7).

Chapter **I**

The Purpose and Use of This Book

This book grew initially out of very personal needs. Our lives have often lacked the discipline of prayer. Despite the fact that we are both involved professionally in the church, we have frequently found ourselves attempting to pray on Sunday mornings without the foundation of a regular life of prayer, with predictably distressing results.

Our experience, we suspect, is not unusual. Many Christians find themselves coming to Sunday services "spiritually rusty." They long for the discipline of daily prayer in which God is praised for the miracle of each new day and acknowledged each day as the center of their lives, but they don't quite know where or how to begin. Left to their own resources, they find the habit of prayer difficult to sustain.

This may be especially true for those Protestants—including members of our denomination, the Christian Church (Disciples of Christ)—whose emphasis on spontaneity in worship has made them suspicious of prescribed "offices" of prayer. Even those individual Protestants who have ventured into *The Divine Office* of the Roman Catholic Church, or into the various forms of morning and evening prayer offered in the Anglican communion, often find themselves in territory that feels too formal and complex.

This book is intended for such persons. It embodies our efforts to develop a pattern of daily prayer that combines the discipline of a daily office with the simple, contemporary yet biblical language of much Protestant spirituality.

Convictions Regarding Prayer

It is clear that Christians have a strong biblical mandate for regular prayer. Jesus not only urges his followers to frequent prayer, he gives them the example. The early Christian community, according to Acts, made regular prayer a central characteristic of its common life. Paul exhorts the Thessalonians to "pray constantly," giving thanks to God in all the times and places of their lives. And Christians throughout the centuries have responded by developing patterns of regular prayer—not simply for their own sakes but because God is great and worthy to be praised.

Still, many Christians today remain suspicious of prayers and readings set forth in ordered sequence. Doesn't this restrict, they ask, the impulse to genuine praise? Doesn't this presume to tame and channel the activity of the Spirit by bringing it under the guidance of the church? Doesn't it limit the freedom of individual believers to worship how and when they will?

We are convinced that some of these suspicions are based on misunderstandings about the nature and purpose of prayer. We undertook this project, quite foreign to our own theological and liturgical backgrounds, because we have come to hold the following convictions:

1. Prayer is not simply a matter of the emotions; it involves the whole person—heart, soul, mind, and strength. It includes thought—careful, sustained reflection on the message of scripture and the lessons of experience. It also involves an act of the will. While God's initiative may lead us into spontaneous acts of praise, prayer is normally something we decide to do, something that can be worked at and improved with practice. Yes, we believe that God hears halting prayers as well as polished ones, but our capacity and desire to turn to God in prayer grows through the discipline of regular praying.

This, of course, is where a daily "office"—a book of regular, suggested (if not prescribed) prayer—comes in. Many Christians seem to think that prayer is not possible unless the feelings are stirred to a proper pitch. But what happens when the Spirit doesn't seem to move, when we are emotionally empty? Isn't that when prayer is most necessary? At such moments, a regular discipline of prayers and readings proves its value.

And, beyond all that, the scriptural injunction to praise God when you sit and when you walk, when you lie down and when you rise, is not dependent on the state of our emotions! Stephen Winward, in his introduction to a daily office written by an ecumenical commission in Great Britain, says it plainly.

. . . the responsible citizen discharges the duties of his office and the trustworthy worker goes to the office whether he feels like it or not. To worship God is an obligation to be discharged irrespective of the presence or absence of feeling. The office [of daily prayer] is the embodiment of this intention, this determination to praise and pray with disciplined regularity. [1]

2. While prayer may be "private," it is never properly understood as "individual." In other words, the public worship of the church is not a collection of individual prayers; our "individual prayers" are, rather, extensions of the church's corporate offering of praise and intercession. The widespread tendency to think of faith and worship as an affair "between me and God," quite divorced from the body of Christ or the world God has created, is surely one of the cardinal heresies of our age.

It is our hope that the prayers in this book will be used by families or larger groups who daily come together to worship God; but we are also aware that this is not always possible. And that is precisely why the traditional pattern of psalms, scripture, and intercessions is so significant. When we read from the canon of scripture, when we join our voices in the recitation of the psalms, when we pray *"Our* Father," when we acknowledge our responsibility to pray for our brothers and sisters, then we are strengthening the ties that bind us. Even if alone, we are united through these words and acts in the ceaseless praise offered by Christians throughout time and space. "I'm fed up," writes Basil Moss in his book *Spirituality for Today,*

11

with this ghastly picture of prayer as a private telephone line with or without a voice at the other end. It's much more like you and me playing our second fiddles in an unending heavenly orchestral symphony of praise and joy. When we pray, we take up our fiddles, and when we stop we put them down again—but the music never stops.[2]

Yes, God has made each one of us as unique individuals; and each of us has a unique responsibility before God that cannot simply be laid on the community. But our distinctiveness must always be seen against the backdrop of the whole church, the whole human family, the whole creation of which we are but a part. We come to know ourselves truly only in relation to the whole.

3. Closely related is the tendency, when left to our own devices, to pray mostly for ourselves. Prayer *should* lay our deepest longings and concerns before God, but, in so doing, it should help expand our range of empathy—beyond ourselves, our families, our congregations, our denominations, our nations to include the whole of creation that God has called good and for which Christ died. This is why a regular cycle of prayer that proposes intercessions for society, the world, and the universal church is so important. Prayer of this sort is an act of the imagination. It forces us to imagine the sufferings and joys of those in other places and other circumstances until they become our own. It helps us to imagine the world as God would have it.

The purpose of prayer, understood in this way, is not simply personal spiritual growth (though that should be a by-product). It is a corporate act of the church on behalf of all creation. In commending the world to God's gracious care, we are participating, in ways we do not fully understand, in God's reconciling work.

Daily Prayer in the History of the Church

The history of daily prayer among Christians is complex and, at least with regard to the early centuries, somewhat uncertain. Still, it is important to identify the basic contours of this history in order to place this book in a wider context.

Early Christian worship borrowed directly and heavily from

first-century Jewish practices. For example, worship in Jewish synagogues included psalmody (the singing of the psalms), the reading of scripture, a sermon, and prayer—all of which quickly became prominent features of Christian services. Both communities recalled God's gracious acts, rejoiced in God with song, and gave thanks to God through prayer.

Christianity also inherited from Judaism a strong tradition of personal or family prayer in the home. Devout Jews offered prayers of praise and petition three times a day, following both the example of scripture—and he got "down on his knees three times a day to pray to his God and praise him" (Daniel 6:10)—and the pattern of sacrifice in the temple. In addition, thanksgiving was offered when one got up in the morning and went to bed at night. The line between public and private is not always clear, however, in accounts of this practice. On the Sabbath, the times of daily prayer became public synagogue services that, by the end of the first century, were extended to weekdays as well.

The earliest-known "manual" of Christian worship, the *Didache* or *Teaching of the Twelve Apostles*, apparently draws on traditional Jewish practice when it advises Christians to pray the Lord's Prayer three times a day. Various church fathers from the second and third centuries also recommended three times for prayer each day "in addition of course to our obligatory prayers which without any command are due at the coming in of daylight and night" (Tertullian). Such prayer could be in community, with one's family, or alone; but even if alone, it was understood to be part of the prayer of the church. According to Cyprian, bishop of Carthage,

> Before all things the teacher of peace and master of unity would not have prayer to be made singly and individually, so that when one prays, he does not pray for himself alone. ... Our prayer is public and common, and when we pray, we pray not for one, but for the whole people, because we that whole people are one. ...[3]

The most important document yet discovered on worship in the third century—the *Apostolic Tradition*, by the Roman writer Hippolytus—describes seven hours of the day for private prayer, stemming perhaps from Psalm 119:64 "Seven times a day I praise thee for thy righteous ordinances." Hippolytus also refers to a daily gathering of the community for instruction, praise, and common prayer. By the fourth century, these daily public services were offered in the major churches of cities throughout the "Christian world." According to a late fourth-century text from Syria, these services consisted of selected psalms, bidding prayers (in which the community is asked to pray for a series of concerns and needs), and a blessing. Private devotion was by no means discouraged, but it was understood to find fuller expression in the daily public worship of the church. Augustine (354-430) writes that "Day by day I rise, go to church, sing there a morning and an evening hymn, and sing a third and fourth in my house. Thus each day I bring a sacrifice of praise and offer it before my God."[4]

This scheme of non-sacramental worship services, celebrated at intervals during the day and night, has generally been termed the "divine office" or, in some traditions, the "daily office." (The word "office" stems from the Latin *officium* meaning "service" or "duty.") The public devotions of the whole church described above are often referred to as the "cathedral office" because they were held in the major church—the cathedral—of a city.

Even as the cathedral office was being developed, however, a movement was underway—monasticism—that eventually would lead to the disappearance of such daily public prayer. Prayer was the dominant activity of monastic communities, and new forms of prayer were soon developed to fit this pattern of disciplined life. The "monastic office" did not use selected psalms but chanted the entire collection in the course of a week (or, in some cases, in the course of a day or even a single service!). This office also read systematically through the whole scripture instead of selecting particular portions of it. Finally, monastic life led to a new and rich collection of formalized prayers, responsories (responses sung in alternation following a reading), and other worship materials.

Early monastic communities followed various schedules for daily prayer until, in the sixth century, Benedict set forth a pattern used by the Roman Catholic Church until the 1960s. The Benedictine rule called for prayer eight times during the day and night: daybreak, shortly thereafter, mid-morning, noon, mid-afternoon, end of the working day, before bedtime, and middle of the night.

The essential point is that the biblical admonition to "pray without ceasing" was gradually understood to be the province of special religious communities and of clergy—with disastrous consequences for the discipline of daily public prayer among "ordinary Christians." James White sums up this development (using a quotation from E. C. Ratcliff) in his *Introduction to Christian Worship*:

> Increasingly the divine office moved away from identification with the secular life of the laity. Monasticism set the tone for this type of worship, and it was imitated by parochial clergy who said the offices daily in the chancels of their empty churches.
> ... Clergy were obliged to follow it [the monastic office]; laity were free to ignore it. And ignore it they did, so that "the offices ceased to be in practice, if not in theory, the common prayer of the Christian people." [5]

In the Protestant Reformation, much of the devotional function of the divine office was shifted to the home—which has had the effect of reinforcing the modern tendency toward individualism in matters of spirituality. Martin Luther did propose a return to two daily services with lessons, psalms, hymns, the Lord's Prayer, collects (short prayers for the day), the creed, and preaching; but the suggestion generated little response.

The major Protestant revision was accomplished by Archbishop Cranmer of the Anglican communion in the sixteenth century. Cranmer reduced the eight services to one in the morning and one in the evening, and encouraged lay participation. The office he devised is composed of psalms (read through each month), scripture (read through in sequence), the Lord's Prayer, canticles (brief hymns from scripture), the creed, and collects. This pattern, or some variation, eventually constituted the regular Sunday service in several Protestant traditions, but it was less successful in restoring the practice of regular daily worship.

Apart from Anglicanism, much Protestant worship has deliberately sought to free itself from prescribed forms such as the divine office. Prayer is certainly encouraged, but it takes the form of freely formulated private devotions that may or may not come at regular intervals and may or may not have much regard for the wider church community.

This, however, is not the end of the story. One of the outstanding developments of this century within Christianity is a renewed interest in worship and spirituality, which has led many Protestants to a deeper appreciation of the church and its discipline of

15

prayer and many Catholics to a higher regard for simplicity and lay participation. The primary case in point is the thorough reform of the divine office mandated by the Roman Catholic Church's Second Vatican Council (1962-65). A new divine office (also now known as *The Liturgy of the Hours*), published in English in 1976, identifies morning and evening prayer as the "hinges" on which the office turns. The basic pattern includes canticles, psalmody (distributed over a four-week cycle), scripture, and intercessions, along with various responses and short prayers.

In his book, *Daily Prayer in the Early Church*, Paul Bradshaw draws four conclusions from his study of this history: (1) The real aim of daily prayer is communion with God. Set hours of prayer are a means to that end and may properly vary in accordance with the spiritual needs and settings of those involved. (2) The heart of these services in the early church was prayer, especially intercessory prayer for the church and the world. (3) Thus, while the psalms have always played a role in the church's services of prayer, they should not be seen as the dominant element. The discipline of reading all of the psalms is a monastic innovation; other principles of selection may appropriately be used. (4) Scripture has been used in various ways in the history of daily prayer and the divine office. Reading it from Genesis to Revelation is one method, but selecting certain texts that address the spiritual needs of the people is also a valid possibility. Bradshaw, along with numerous other scholars, encourages renewal of the daily office by moving beyond the patterns inherited from monastic life to ones more appropriate for the whole of the contemporary church. [6]

A Recommended Pattern of Daily Prayer

This book draws on the traditions of both private devotion and the daily office. The basic pattern we recommend—psalms, readings, and prayers of thanksgiving and intercession—is essentially that found in *The Daily Office* of the Anglican communion or *The Divine Office* of the Roman Catholic Church; but we have streamlined and adapted it in ways that may feel more familiar to persons from churches with less formal worship traditions. The idea is not to make spiritual discipline "easier" but to provide a tool for those individuals, families, and groups who have not previously developed the habit of daily prayer. Our hope is that the materials in this book are both consistent with the church's great tradition of regular prayer and accessible for those unfamiliar with that tradition.

Chapter II presents a four-week cycle of daily readings and prayers. The materials suggested for each day have four essential elements:

1. *Opening Prayer.* This brief prayer lifts up the dominant theme of all Christian worship: thankful praise to God who has loved us so fully. Each of the twenty-eight prayers offered in Chapter II expresses this theme with images and language drawn from the readings for that particular day, especially the reading from the psalms. It is also appropriate that many of these prayers confess our sinfulness before God. We know that we have fallen short of God's intention for our lives; but each new day reminds us of the miracle of forgiveness and renewal that is possible through the God who was in Christ. God's word of gracious love inevitably pronounces judgment on our prideful allegiance to lesser things. But because it is God's word, it remains good news—and our response is one of thankful praise.

This opening prayer is actually a departure from most patterns of the daily office, which open with readings from the psalms and move to prayer following scripture. It has been helpful for us, however, to establish from the outset both the focus and theme of our devotional time by directly giving thanks to God.

2. *Reading from the Psalms.* As we have seen, the psalms have been a central part of the church's daily prayer from the early centuries. Reading these wonderful songs of praise helps link our prayers, even if uttered alone, to the corporate worship of the church around the world and across the generations. It also roots our prayer in the life of Israel for whom the psalms were a primary language of devotion.

Traditionally, religious communities have read through all 150 psalms in the course of a week, a month, or other regular interval. We certainly commend this practice. Read in their entirety, the psalms expose us to an incredible range of emotion—wonder, fear, frustration, trust, resignation, joy, hope—which gives depth and meaning to our experience before God. We have decided, however, to make selective use of the psalms for our four-week cycle, choosing those that pay central attention to the themes of praise and thanksgiving. This is intended as an introduction, a taste of these scriptural treasures. Once persons have established the rhythm of daily reading, they may wish to incorporate all of the psalms in their devotional practice.

On Sunday of each week, we have replaced the psalm with a reading from Isaiah that lifts up the vision of that day when God's shalom shall prevail over all the earth. Christians live both by memory and anticipation. We give thanks not only for what God has done but for what God has promised to do for our salvation.

The readings in this book are from the New Revised Standard Version, published by the National Council of Churches of Christ. This text is likely to replace the RSV as the basic ecumenical translation. It also has the advantage of greater inclusiveness, especially in its references to humanity. Fully inclusive translations of the psalms are also available.

3. *Reading from the New Testament.* Central to our life as a community of faith is the witness of the apostles, as recorded in scripture, to God's gracious works, especially in Jesus Christ. Prayer is a response to the loving initiative of God to which the Bible testifies. Yet how frequently this witness is ignored, even by those who pay lip service to its authority!

Part of the purpose of an office of daily readings and prayers is to expose us to the breadth and depth of the biblical story. We are enjoined in Deuteronomy to teach this story to ourselves and our children when we are sitting in our house, when we are walking by the way, when we lie down, and when we rise—until the message of God's love seeps into our bones and determines the very way we see reality. Thus, as with the psalms, a reading of the entire New Testament—indeed, of the entire Bible—is recommended. Communities that use a daily office organize it around a "lectionary" or systematic listing of biblical passages. We have included an ecumenically-produced lectionary for this purpose in Chapter III.

In the four-week cycle that follows, however, we have felt the need to be selective and have made our selections according to the theme of reconciliation. More specifically, the readings for Monday and Thursday lift up the theme of reconciliation with God, those on Tuesday and Friday speak to the issue of reconciliation with neighbor, while the texts for Wednesday and Saturday focus on reconciliation within the church. (These distinctions are not easy to maintain, since many of the New Testament passages that speak of relationships with others are actually about the structuring of the new community in Christ. The idea of reconciliation, however, should be apparent throughout.)

We selected the theme of reconciliation both because it is at the heart of the gospel and because it seems of particular importance in contemporary society. The daily headlines confirm the insight of St. Augustine that human beings are "curved in" on themselves. We trust in our wealth, our weapons, our intelligence, our creativity and, thus, are unable to trust finally or fully in God, the One in whom we truly live and move and have our being. And, scripture tells us, there is nothing we can do on our own to restore this broken relationship. No matter how high our IQ, no matter how many people we "convert," no matter how much money we give for refugees, no matter how many prayers we say, we cannot reconcile ourselves to God.

That, however, is where the good news begins. The readings we have selected do not teach us how to draw near to God; rather, they give witness that God has drawn near to us. The promise is this: If we accept God's act of grace in Jesus Christ, if we receive this gift through faith, if we begin to experience ourselves as freed, forgiven children of God, then our very lives are transformed. Instead of being curved in, our lives face out toward God's image in our neighbors. Instead of being anxious about how much we can accumulate or whether or not we get our fair share, we give constant thanks for what we have been given. Instead of living lives cramped by the need for self-confirmation, we live lives of gratitude in response to grace. Daily prayer, understood in light of this witness, does not "create" communion with God; it is a response to God's reconciling initiative.

The readings we have chosen also lift up another side of this message: Reconciliation with God means reconciliation with our sisters and brothers in the human family who are also children of the one Creator. Jesus taught two commandments and they are completely intertwined. We love God in and through the neighbor, and we love the neighbor because we know ourselves to be loved by God. In this sense, Christians do not have special privileges but special responsibilities. "So we are ambassadors for Christ, God appealing through us" (2 Corinthians 5:20).

4. *Intercessory Prayer.* Intercessory prayer—prayer that appeals to God on behalf of other persons or creation—is an essential trait of Christian life and, from the beginning, has been given a prominent place in Christian worship. The Bible records how Abraham, Moses, and the prophets repeatedly interceded with God for the people of Israel. Jesus prayed for others, including his disciples, in

the "high priestly prayer" of John 17 and for his persecutors from the cross. And, in a larger sense, the Incarnation is, itself, an act of intercession through which Jesus Christ bore the burdens of others, giving up his life for the world. From Paul (Romans 8:34) to the present, Christians have confessed that the risen Lord continues to intercede for humanity.

As followers of Christ, we participate in his redemptive work by strengthening our bonds within the church and the wider human community through prayer. There is a temptation to thank God that we have blessings others may not enjoy. Intercessory prayer opens us to the needs of others and is, thus, an expression of love; but it is also a prelude to more direct forms of acting. Our prayer is, in part, that God will strengthen us to act on behalf of those for whom we pray.

Intercessory prayer is something we do but it is also something that God does through us. Paul expresses this in Romans 8:26 when he writes that " . . . the Spirit helps us in our weakness; for we do not know how to pray as we ought, but that very Spirit intercedes with sighs too deep for words." In daily prayer we open ourselves to the movement of God's spirit, in part through our praise and thanksgiving. Having given thanks to God for what God has done in our lives and the life of the world, we also remember God's promises and pray that these may be fulfilled, especially in the lives of those who suffer. Thanksgiving leads naturally to intercession; but intercession begins in thanksgiving lest we concentrate more on needs than gifts.

These moments are the time to place before God our deepest hopes, anxieties, or concerns. If a loved one is ill, he or she should certainly be lifted up in prayer. But as believers in a universal God and members of a universal church, we must not restrict our prayers to our family, our circle of friends, our congregation. *The Book of Common Prayer* suggests that prayer be offered with intercession for

—the universal church, its members and mission,
—the nation and all in authority,
—the welfare of the world,
—the concerns of the local community,
—those who suffer and those in any trouble,
—the departed.

20

The four-week cycle in this book recommends themes for which you might pray in order to help you begin and as a reminder to maintain this breadth of focus. These suggestions relate, in a general way, to the reading from the New Testament (e.g., on Wednesday, the intercessions give special attention to the church and pray for the reconciliation of its parts). The real focus of these moments, however, is up to you.

Suggestions for Using This Book

The prayers and readings found in Chapter II are generally written for use in the morning, but can be easily adapted for evening or any time in between. Please note that the prayers will take on a different character at different times of the day.

Morning prayer is a way of dedicating the day to God, of centering our often hectic and petty lives on that which is true and eternal. Dietrich Bonhoeffer puts it just right:

> Common life under the Word begins with common worship at the beginning of the day . . . . For Christians, the beginning of the day should not be burdened and oppressed with besetting concerns for the day's work. At the threshold of the new day stands the Lord who made it. All the darkness and distraction of the dreams of night retreat before the clear light of Jesus Christ and his wakening word. All unrest, all impurity, all care and anxiety flee before him. Therefore, at the beginning of the day let all distraction and empty talk be silenced and let the first thought and first word belong to him to whom our whole life belongs. [7]

The morning itself provides obvious, but still powerful, images for prayer. The rising sun, source of warmth and light, brings to mind the One we confess as Risen Lord. The new day, in which that which is old seems truly put behind, reminds us of God who makes all things new.

If your prayer is offered at the beginning of the day, it can also serve as a plumb line for the hours that follow. In moments of anger or anxiety, try recalling the images of the psalm, the vision of the reading, or the spirit of the prayers. Develop the discipline of relating events throughout the day to these opening moments when your life is placed before God.

Evening prayer, though also for the fundamental purpose of giving thankful praise to God, has a different tone. At the close of the day, we offer thanks for its blessings but also ask pardon for the ways we have offended against God and neighbor. Of equal importance, evening is a time to let go of lingering resentments, to stop fingering old wounds, through prayerful remembrance that we are continually blessed beyond all deserving. "Be angry but do not sin; do not let the sun go down on your anger," writes the author of Ephesians. "Put away from you all bitterness and wrath and anger and wrangling and slander, together with all malice, and be kind to one another, tenderhearted, forgiving one another, as God in Christ has forgiven you " (Ephesians 4:26, 31-32).

Not only can the prayers and readings that follow be said at various times, they can be appropriate, in our opinion, in a wide variety of settings. A retired person living alone might begin each day with prayer; a young couple might say the prayers together before their small children are up; families might offer them together before breakfast or after dinner. The cycle of prayers and readings could be used by church staffs or seminary communities before work or classes begin; the pattern could be adapted for retreats or groups of friends who gather regularly for common prayer. The possibilities are numerous. But it must be stressed that daily prayer, whatever its setting, is not a substitute for weekly worship in wider Christian community. If offered by one person or fifty, daily prayer must be seen as an extension of the praise and thanksgiving offered by Christ's one body. Through the discipline of daily prayer, our spiritual lives grow in maturity and scope and, in this way, our participation in the church's corporate worship is enriched.

Individuals or families may wish to begin with the four-week cycle as printed. Once the pattern is familiar, once these readings and prayers become part of the way you understand yourself and the world, start drawing on the materials in Chapter III. Substitute the more comprehensive lectionary for the psalms and New Testament passages suggested in Chapter II. Add the churches listed in the "Ecumenical Prayer Cycle" to your own intercessions. Try concluding the intercessions with the Lord's Prayer and/or one of the "Prayers from the Universal Church" printed in Chapter III.

You may also want to substitute spontaneous prayer, or prayers of your own composition, for the opening prayers we provide.

Groups may wish to use an expanded pattern from the start. The following is one possibility for a service of morning or evening prayer.

Greeting (call to worship)

> A refrain taken from the day's psalm, which may be used for this purpose, is provided for each day of our recommended cycle. The "invitatory psalms" printed in Chapter III are also intended as openings for daily prayer.

Opening Prayer

> This could, of course, be said in unison or by a prayer leader.

Hymn

> If you would prefer not to sing, try saying together one of the "canticles" found in Chapter III. The hymn, optional in any case, may also go after the psalm or the second reading from scripture.

Reading from the Psalms

> Try dividing the group in half and reading the psalm "antiphonally" (i.e., in alternation). Another traditional approach is for the group to repeat a refrain at designated points during the reading. For the psalms printed in Chapter II, we have provided a possible refrain and have indicated with asterisks where the psalm may appropriately be broken for the refrain. These markings also show where the alternation of voices should occur for antiphonal reading.

Reading from the New Testament

> We suggest you start with the readings in Chapter II and then move to the lectionary. Another possibility is to

choose a particular book of the Bible, reading several verses or a chapter each day.

Silent Meditation

Intercessory Prayer

Various responsive forms of prayer, appropriate for groups, are suggested in Chapter III.

Lord's Prayer

Benediction

Again, the printed line from the psalm could be used. Familiar benedictions from scripture include Numbers 6:24-26; 2 Corinthians 13:14; 1 Corinthians 16:13-14; and Philippians 4:7. Alternatively, you may want to use a constant formulation, e.g.,

Leader: Go in peace to love and serve the Lord.
Response: Thanks be to God.

These suggestions and the materials that follow are in no sense prescriptive. Once the habit of prayer is established, be creative! Corporate worship may follow formal patterns (at least in some churches) but, as Cheslyn Jones puts it, in matters of spirituality there are no "rules of the game" but only "tips of the trade."[8] May these "tips" be of use to you and may the prayers they stimulate be to the glory of God!

This is the day which the Lord has made; let us rejoice and be glad in it
(Psalm 118:24).

Do not worry about anything, but in everything by prayer and supplication with thanksgiving let your requests be made known to God
(Philippians 4:6).

Chapter **II**
A Four-Week Cycle of Daily Readings and Prayers

Table of Readings

WEEK I

Monday	Psalm 8	2 Corinthians 5:14-21
Tuesday	Psalm 16	Matthew 5:21-26, 43-48
Wednesday	Psalm 19:1-10, 14	Ephesians 2:11-22
Thursday	Psalm 23	Luke 15:11-24
Friday	Psalm 32	Luke 10:25-37
Saturday	Psalm 33:1-12, 16-22	James 2:1-13
Sunday	Isaiah 2:1-4	Mark 6:30-44

WEEK II

Monday	Psalm 46	Romans 5:1-11
Tuesday	Psalm 51:1-17	1 Corinthians 13:1-13
Wednesday	Psalm 65	Colossians 3:9-17
Thursday	Psalm 84	Galatians 4:1-9
Friday	Psalm 89:1-16	Matthew 18:21-35
Saturday	Psalm 96	1 Corinthians 12:12-26
Sunday	Isaiah 11:1-9	Hebrews 10:11-25

WEEK III

Monday	Psalm 97	Colossians 1:15-23a
Tuesday	Psalm 98	Romans 12:9-21
Wednesday	Psalm 103:1-18	Ephesians 4:1-7, 11-16
Thursday	Psalm 104:1-15	John 4:7-15
Friday	Psalm 104:24-35	2 Timothy 3:14—4:5
Saturday	Psalm 119:1-16	John 17:20-26
Sunday	Isaiah 55:6-13	Matthew 26:17-29

WEEK IV

Monday	Psalm 121	Romans 8:31-39
Tuesday	Psalm 139:1-15, 23-24	1 John 4:7-21
Wednesday	Psalm 145:1-16, 21	1 Corinthians 1:10-13; 3:1-9
Thursday	Psalm 146	Philippians 2:1-13
Friday	Psalm 147:1-15, 19-20	Luke 4:16-30
Saturday	Psalm 148	1 Peter 2:1-10
Sunday	Isaiah 65:17-25	Luke 24:13-20, 28-35

WEEK I — Monday

Reconciliation with God

Opening Prayer: O God, our God, how glorious is your name in all the earth! We marvel at the variety and goodness of your creation and give thanks that we are part of all you have made. Most of all we offer thanks for the gift of reconciliation through Jesus Christ in whom we are forgiven and made new. Strengthen us now, by your Holy Spirit, that this day may find us living not only for ourselves but as ambassadors of your reconciling love. In Christ's name we pray. Amen.

Reading from the Psalms   Psalm 8

(The asterisks [*] indicate where the refrain may be repeated or where the psalm may be broken for antiphonal reading. See page 21.)
Refrain: O Lord, how majestic is your name in all the earth!

O LORD, our Sovereign,
    how majestic is your name in all the earth!

You have set your glory above the heavens.
    Out of the mouths of babes and infants
you have founded a bulwark because of your foes,
    to silence the enemy and the avenger.

When I look at your heavens, the work of your fingers,
    the moon and the stars that you have established;
what are human beings that you are mindful of them,
    mortals that you care for them?*

Yet you have made them a little lower than God,
    and crowned them with glory and honor.
You have given them dominion over the works of your
        hands;
    you have put all things under their feet,
all sheep and oxen,
    and also the beasts of the field,
the birds of the air, and the fish of the sea,
    whatever passes along the paths of the seas.

O LORD, our Sovereign,
    how majestic is your name in all the earth!

Reading from the New Testament   2 Corinthians 5:14-21

For the love of Christ urges us on, because we are convinced that one has died for all; therefore all have died. And he died for all, so that those who live might live no longer for themselves, but for him who died and was raised for them.

From now on, therefore, we regard no one from a human point of view; even though we once knew Christ from a human point of view, we know him no longer in that way. So if anyone is in Christ, there is a new creation: everything old has passed away; see, everything has become new! All this is from God, who reconciled us to himself through Christ, and has given us the ministry of reconciliation; that is, in Christ God was reconciling the world to himself, not counting their trespasses against them, and entrusting the message of reconciliation to us. So we are ambassadors for Christ, since God is making his appeal through us; we entreat you on behalf of Christ, be reconciled to God. For our sake he made him to be sin who knew no sin, so that in him we might become the righteousness of God.

Intercessions: We pray this day
—for those who live without hope or knowledge of God.
—for creation and for the will to protect that which God has made and entrusted to our care.

WEEK I —Tuesday

Reconciliation with Neighbor

Opening Prayer: We come to you in the morning's quiet, dear God, giving thanks for this time of prayer. The new day, with its possibilities and hopes, reminds us that we have no good apart from you. Yet how often we waste that which you provide through self-centered living. Forgive us, most perfect Creator. Renew us this day by your Spirit that we may be slow to find fault and quick to show love, slow to condemn and quick to forgive. Guide us into the lives of others—neighbor and enemy, stranger and friend— that together we may give you glory. Amen.

Reading from the Psalms   Psalm 16

Refrain: In your presence there is fullness of joy.

Protect me, O God, for in you I take refuge.
I say to the LORD, "You are my Lord;
   I have no good apart from you."*

As for the holy ones in the land, they are the noble,
   in whom is all my delight.

Those who choose another god multiply their sorrows;
   their drink offerings of blood I will not pour out
   or take their names upon my lips.*

The LORD is my chosen portion and my cup;
   you hold my lot.
The boundary lines have fallen for me in pleasant places;
   I have a goodly heritage.

I bless the LORD who gives me counsel;
   in the night also my heart instructs me.
I keep the LORD always before me;
   because he is at my right hand, I shall not be moved.*

Therefore my heart is glad, and my soul rejoices;
   my body also rests secure.
For you do not give me up to Sheol,
   or let your faithful one see the Pit.

You show me the path of life.
   In your presence there is fullness of joy;
   In your right hand are pleasures forevermore.

Reading from the New Testament Matthew 5:21-26, 43-48

"You have heard that it was said to those of ancient times, 'You shall not murder'; and 'whoever murders shall be liable to judgment.' But I say to you that if you are angry with a brother or sister, you will be liable to judgment; and if you insult a brother or sister, you will be liable to the council; and if you say, 'You fool,' you will be liable to the hell of fire. So when you are offering your gift at the altar, if you remember that your brother or sister has something against you, leave your gift there before the altar and go; first be reconciled to your brother or sister, and then come and offer your gift. Come to terms quickly with your accuser while you are on the way to court with him, or your accuser may hand you over to the judge, and the judge to the guard, and you will be thrown into prison. Truly I tell you, you will never get out until you have paid the last penny."

"You have heard that it was said, 'You shall love your neighbor and hate your enemy.' But I say to you, Love your enemies and pray for those who persecute you, so that you may be children of your Father in heaven; for he makes his sun rise on the evil and on the good, and sends rain on the righteous and on the unrighteous. For if you love those who love you, what reward do you have? Do not even the tax collectors do the same? And if you greet only your brothers and sisters, what more are you doing than others? Do not even the Gentiles do the same? Be perfect, therefore, as your heavenly Father is perfect."

Intercessions: We pray this day
—for those with whom we are not reconciled.
—that the church may be an agent of reconciliation in situations of conflict around the world.

WEEK I —Wednesday

Reconciliation Within the Church

Opening Prayer: The rising sun proclaims the news: You are the Holy One, the giver of life, the just and loving Creator of all that is. Your law, O God, is perfect, your rule is trustworthy, your command is clear. We rejoice that through Jesus Christ we are no longer strangers to your promise but members of your household. Yet we have made your church too small, a series of walls and chambers that divide the body of Christ. We have used the cross to separate rather than unite. Forgive us, faithful God, and renew our desire for unity. Urgently call us back to him who is our peace, the cornerstone in whom we are one and in whose name we pray. Amen.

Reading from the Psalms   Psalm 19:1-10, 14

Refrain: The law of the Lord is perfect, reviving the soul.

The heavens are telling the glory of God;
    and the firmament proclaims his handiwork.
Day to day pours forth speech,
    and night to night declares knowledge.
There is no speech, nor are there words;
    their voice is not heard;
yet their voice goes out through all the earth,
    and their words to the end of the world.*

In the heavens he has set a tent for the sun,
which comes out like a bridegroom from his wedding
      canopy,
    and like a strong man runs its course with joy.
Its rising is from the end of the heavens,
    and its circuit to the end of them;
    and nothing is hid from its heat.

The law of the LORD is perfect,
    reviving the soul;
the decrees of the LORD are sure,
    making wise the simple;
the precepts of the LORD are right,
    rejoicing the heart;
the commandment of the LORD is clear,
    enlightening the eyes;
the fear of the LORD is pure,
    enduring forever;
the ordinances of the LORD are true
    and righteous altogether.*
More to be desired are they than gold,
    even much fine gold;
sweeter also than honey,
    and drippings of the honeycomb.

Let the words of my mouth and the meditation of my
    heart
    be acceptable to you,
    O LORD, my rock and my redeemer.*

Reading from the New Testament   Ephesians 2:11-22

So then, remember that at one time you Gentiles by birth, called
"the uncircumcision" by those who are called "the circumcision"—
a physical circumcision made in the flesh by human hands—
remember that you were at that time without Christ, being aliens

from the commonwealth of Israel, and strangers to the covenants of promise, having no hope and without God in the world. But now in Christ Jesus you who once were far off have been brought near by the blood of Christ. For he is our peace; in his flesh he has made both groups into one and has broken down the dividing wall, that is, the hostility between us. He has abolished the law with its commandments and ordinances, that he might create in himself one new humanity in place of the two, thus making peace, and might reconcile both groups to God in one body through the cross, thus putting to death that hostility through it. So he came and proclaimed peace to you who were far off and peace to those who were near; for through him both of us have access in one Spirit to the Father. So then you are no longer strangers and aliens, but you are citizens with the saints and also members of the household of God, built upon the foundation of the apostles and prophets, with Christ Jesus himself as the cornerstone. In him the whole structure is joined together and grows into a holy temple in the Lord; in whom you also are built together spiritually into a dwelling place for God.

Intercessions: We pray this day
—that the Spirit of God will teach the church to distinguish between the richness of diversity and the sinfulness of division.
—for nations in which walls of hostility divide persons of different races, cultures, and religions.

WEEK I —Thursday

Reconciliation with God

Opening Prayer: Great Shepherd, who comforts us in times of need— forgiving Parent, who welcomes us back if we will but turn to you —we praise and glorify your name for the wonder of this new day. Remind us, in these moments of prayer, that it is your goodness and mercy that fill the days of our lives, that it is you beside us in times of darkness. Enable us, in turn, to comfort as we have been comforted, to forgive as we have been forgiven, and to love as we have been loved. We pray it in the name of our Savior, Jesus Christ. Amen.

Reading from the Psalms   Psalm 23

Refrain: The Lord is my shepherd, I shall not want.

The LORD is my shepherd, I shall not want.
   He makes me lie down in green pastures;
he leads me beside still waters;
   he restores my soul.
He leads me in right paths
   for his name's sake.*

Even though I walk through the darkest valley,
   I fear no evil;
for you are with me;
   your rod and your staff —
   they comfort me.*

You prepare a table before me
   in the presence of my enemies;
you anoint my head with oil;
   my cup overflows.
Surely goodness and mercy shall follow me
   all the days of my life,
and I shall dwell in the house of the LORD
   my whole life long.*

Reading from the New Testament   Luke 15:11-24

Then Jesus said, "There was a man who had two sons. The younger of them said to his father, 'Father, give me the share of the property that will belong to me.' So he divided his property between them. A few days later the younger son gathered all he had and traveled to a distant country, and there he squandered his property in dissolute living. When he had spent everything, a severe famine took place throughout that country, and he began to be in need. So he went and hired himself out to one of the citizens of that country, who sent him to his fields to feed the pigs. He would gladly have filled himself with the pods that the pigs were eating; and no one gave him anything. But when he came to himself he said, 'How many of my father's hired hands have bread enough and to spare, but here I am dying of hunger! I will get up and go to my father, and I will say to him, "Father, I have sinned against heaven and before you; I am no longer worthy to be called your son;

treat me like one of your hired hands."' So he set off and went to his father. But while he was still far off, his father saw him and was filled with compassion; he ran and put his arms around him and kissed him. Then the son said to him, 'Father, I have sinned against heaven and before you; I am no longer worthy to be called your son.' But the father said to his slaves, 'Quickly, bring out a robe—the best one—and put it on him; put a ring on his finger and sandals on his feet. And get the fatted calf and kill it, and let us eat and celebrate; for this son of mine was dead and is alive again; he was lost and is found!' And they began to celebrate."

Intercessions: We pray this day
   —that all who are fearful and in need may trust in God as the one sure source of goodness and mercy.
   —for children who lack a parent's love.

WEEK I —Friday

Reconciliation with Neighbor

Opening Prayer: Merciful God, great deliverer, we come before you at the beginning of this day chastened in the knowledge of our sinfulness. We have not loved you with all our heart, soul, strength, and mind; we have not loved our neighbors as ourselves. But we also come before you filled with the wonder of your gracious love. Blessed are we whose sins are forgiven! Strengthen us, we pray, to respond with acts of compassion. Teach us to see, within the humanity of our neighbors, the miracle of your image. Through Christ we pray. Amen.

Reading from the Psalms   Psalm 32

Refrain: Let all who are faithful offer prayer to you.

   Happy are those whose transgression is forgiven,
     whose sin is covered.
   Happy are those to whom the LORD imputes no iniquity,
     and in whose spirit there is no deceit.*

While I kept silence, my body wasted away
   through my groaning all day long.
For day and night your hand was heavy upon me;
   my strength was dried up as by the heat of summer.*

Then I acknowledged my sin to you,
   and I did not hide my iniquity;
I said, "I will confess my transgressions to the LORD,"
   and you forgave the guilt of my sin.

Therefore let all who are faithful
   offer prayer to you;
at a time of distress, the rush of mighty waters
   shall not reach them.
You are a hiding place for me;
   you preserve me from trouble;
   you surround me with glad cries of deliverance.*

I will instruct you and teach you the way you should go;
   I will counsel you with my eye upon you.
Do not be like a horse or a mule, without understanding,
   whose temper must be curbed with bit and bridle,
   else it will not stay near you.*

Many are the torments of the wicked,
   but steadfast love surrounds those who trust in the
      LORD.
Be glad in the LORD and rejoice, O righteous,
   and shout for joy, all you upright in heart.

Reading from the New Testament   Luke 10:25-37

/ Just then a lawyer stood up to test Jesus. "Teacher," he said,
"what must I do to inherit eternal life?" He said to him, "What is
written in the law? What do you read there?" He answered, "You
shall love the Lord your God with all your heart, and with all your
soul, and with all your strength, and with all your mind; and your
neighbor as yourself." And he said to him, "You have given the
right answer; do this, and you will live."

   But wanting to justify himself, he asked Jesus, "And who is my
neighbor?" Jesus replied, "A man was going down from Jerusalem
to Jericho, and fell into the hands of robbers, who stripped him, beat
him, and went away, leaving him half dead. Now by chance a
priest was going down that road; and when he saw him, he passed
by on the other side. So likewise a Levite, when he came to the place

and saw him, passed by on the other side. But a Samaritan while traveling came near him; and when he saw him, he was moved with pity. He went to him and bandaged his wounds, having poured oil and wine on them. Then he put him on his own animal, brought him to an inn, and took care of him. The next day he took out two denarii, gave them to the innkeeper, and said, 'Take care of him; and when I come back, I will repay you whatever more you spend.' Which of these three, do you think, was a neighbor to the man who fell into the hands of the robbers?" He said, "The one who showed him mercy." Jesus said to him, "Go and do likewise."

Intercessions: We pray this day
—for those left by the wayside without adequate food, help, or shelter, for those who give them aid, for those who pass them by.
—that the church may be faithful to its vocation as agent of God's healing in the world.

WEEK I—Saturday

Reconciliation Within the Church

Opening Prayer: The sounds of morning bring word of your faithful love, holy Creator. We thank you this morning for the ways you have revealed yourself to us: for scripture, which teaches of your righteousness; for creation, which displays your glory; for the church, which shows us the meaning of life in Christ. Truly it is right to sing out our joy that you are God! Forgive us, Lord, when we deny your plan for justice, making distinctions among ourselves. Forgive us when we ignore your counsel, loving our own schemes better. Fashion our hearts that we might be your reconciled people. ~~Amen.~~ AND HEAR US AS WE PRAY...

Reading from the Psalms   Psalm 33:1-12, 16-22

Refrain: Our soul waits for the Lord; God is our help and shield.

Rejoice in the LORD, O you righteous.
　　Praise befits the upright.
Praise the LORD with the lyre;
　　make melody to him with the harp of ten strings.

Sing to him a new song;
    play skillfully on the strings, with loud shouts.*

For the word of the LORD is upright,
    and all his work is done in faithfulness.
He loves righteousness and justice;
    the earth is full of the steadfast love of the LORD.*

By the word of the LORD the heavens were made,
    and all their host by the breath of his mouth.
He gathered the waters of the sea as in a bottle;
    he put the deeps in storehouses.

Let all the earth fear the LORD;
    let all the inhabitants of the world stand in awe of
       him.
For he spoke, and it came to be;
    he commanded, and it stood firm.*

The LORD brings the counsels of the nations to nothing;
    he frustrates the plans of the peoples.
The counsel of the LORD stands forever,
    the thoughts of his heart to all generations.
Happy is the nation whose God is the LORD,
    the people whom he has chosen as his heritage.*

A king is not saved by his great army;
    a warrior is not delivered by his great strength.
The war horse is a vain hope for victory,
    and by its great might it cannot save.*

Truly the eye of the LORD is on those who fear him,
    on those who hope in his steadfast love,
to deliver their soul from death,
    and to keep them alive in famine.*

Our soul waits for the LORD;
    he is our help and shield.
Our heart is glad in him,
    because we trust in his holy name.
Let your steadfast love, O LORD, be upon us,
    even as we hope in you.

Reading from the New Testament   James 2:1-13

    My brothers and sisters, do you with your acts of favoritism really believe in our glorious Lord Jesus Christ? For if a person with gold rings and in fine clothes comes into your assembly, and if a poor person in dirty clothes also comes in, and if you take notice of the one wearing the fine clothes and say, "Have a seat here, please," while to the one who is poor you say, "Stand there," or "Sit at my feet," have you not made distinctions among yourselves, and become judges with evil thoughts? Listen, my beloved brothers and sisters. Has not God chosen the poor in the world to be rich in faith and to be heirs of the kingdom that he has promised to those who love him? But you have dishonored the poor. Is it not the rich who oppress you? Is it not they who drag you into court? Is it not they who blaspheme the excellent name that was invoked over you?

You do well if you really fulfill the royal law according to the scripture, "You shall love your neighbor as yourself." But if you show partiality, you commit sin and are convicted by the law as transgressors. For whoever keeps the whole law but fails in one point has become accountable for all of it. For the one who said, "You shall not commit adultery," also said, "You shall not murder." Now if you do not commit adultery but if you murder, you have become a transgressor of the law. So speak and so act as those who are to be judged by the law of liberty. For judgment will be without mercy to anyone who has shown no mercy; mercy triumphs over judgment.

Intercessions: We pray this day
—for the unity of the church across sinful barriers between rich and poor.
—for those who suffer when the church is unfaithful to God's call for justice.

WEEK I—Sunday

The Lord's Supper

Opening Prayer: Bountiful God, who gathers your church and feeds it through word and sacrament, fill us, we pray, with the joy of your presence. Turn us from lessons of war to lessons of peace. Turn us from a craving for the things of this world to a hunger for that which satisfies forever. We pray, dearest God, that as you have ushered in this Lord's Day so you will usher in that day of your holy realm of peace. Help us to live so that our lives are signs, however small, of its coming. In the name of Christ we pray. Amen.

Reading from the Prophets   Isaiah 2:1-4

The word that Isaiah son of Amoz saw concerning Judah in
    Jerusalem.

In days to come
    the mountain of the LORD'S house
shall be established as the highest of the mountains,
    and shall be raised above the hills;
all the nations shall stream to it.
    Many peoples shall come and say,
"Come, let us go up to the mountain of the LORD,
    to the house of the God of Jacob;
that he may teach us his ways
    and that we may walk in his paths."
For out of Zion shall go forth instruction,
    and the word of the LORD from Jerusalem.
He shall judge between the nations,
    and shall arbitrate for many peoples;
they shall beat their swords into plowshares,
    and their spears into pruning hooks;
nation shall not lift up sword against nation,
    neither shall they learn war any more.

Reading from the New Testament   Mark 6:30-44

The apostles gathered around Jesus, and told him all that they
had done and taught. He said to them, "Come away to a deserted
place all by yourselves and rest a while." For many were coming
and going, and they had no leisure even to eat. And they went
away in the boat to a deserted place by themselves. Now many saw
them going and recognized them, and they hurried there on foot
from all the towns and arrived ahead of them. As he went ashore,
he saw a great crowd; and he had compassion for them, because
they were like sheep without a shepherd; and he began to teach
them many things. When it grew late, his disciples came to him and
said, "This is a deserted place, and the hour is now very late; send
them away so that they may go into the surrounding country and
villages and buy something for themselves to eat." But he answered them, "You give them something to eat." They said to him,
"Are we to go and buy two hundred denarii worth of bread, and
give it to them to eat?" And he said to them, "How many loaves
have you? Go and see." When they had found out, they said, "Five,

and two fish." Then he ordered them to get all the people to sit down in groups on the green grass. So they sat down in groups of hundreds and of fifties. Taking the five loaves and the two fish, he looked up to heaven, and blessed and broke the loaves, and gave them to his disciples to set before the people; and he divided the two fish among them all. And all ate and were filled; and they took up twelve baskets full of broken pieces and of the fish. Those who had eaten the loaves numbered five thousand men.

Intercessions: We pray this day
—for peace among the nations.
—for Christians gathered around the Lord's Table in local communities.

WEEK II — Monday

Reconciliation with God

Opening Prayer: O God, our refuge and our strength, our help in times of need, our hope in times of trouble, we praise you for your marvelous acts of creation and reconciliation: for the beauty of this day, for the love we will experience during it, for the knowledge of your son who comes to us in the midst of our sin and helplessness. No matter how hectic our lives may seem, we pray that they will bear witness to the love you have poured within us. Help us this day to still our anxious souls and know that you alone are God. Amen.

Reading from the Psalms   Psalm 46

(The asterisks [*] indicate where the refrain may be repeated or where the psalm may be broken for antiphonal reading.)

Refrain: God is our refuge and strength, a very present help in trouble.

God is our refuge and strength,
    a very present help in trouble.
Therefore we will not fear, though the earth should
      change,
    though the mountains shake in the heart of the sea;
though its waters roar and foam,
    though the mountains tremble with its tumult.*

There is a river whose streams make glad the city of
      God,
    the holy habitation of the Most High.
God is in the midst of the city; it shall not be moved;
    God will help it when the morning dawns.
The nations are in an uproar, the kingdoms totter;
    he utters his voice, the earth melts.
The LORD of hosts is with us;
    the God of Jacob is our refuge.*

Come, behold the works of the LORD;
    see what desolations he has brought on the earth.
He makes wars cease to the end of the earth;

he breaks the bow, and shatters the spear;
he burns the shields with fire.
"Be still, and know that I am God!
I am exalted among the nations,
I am exalted in the earth."
The LORD of hosts is with us;
the God of Jacob is our refuge.*

Reading from the New Testament — Romans 5:1-11

Therefore, since we are justified by faith, we have peace with God through our Lord Jesus Christ, through whom we have obtained access to this grace in which we stand; and we boast in our hope of sharing the glory of God. And not only that, but we also boast in our sufferings, knowing that suffering produces endurance, and endurance produces character, and character produces hope, and hope does not disappoint us, because God's love has been poured into our hearts through the Holy Spirit that has been given to us.
For while we were still weak, at the right time Christ died for the ungodly. Indeed, rarely will anyone die for a righteous person—though perhaps for a good person someone might actually dare to die. But God proves his love for us in that while we still were sinners Christ died for us. Much more surely then, now that we have been justified by his blood, will we be saved through him from the wrath of God. For if while we were enemies, we were reconciled to God through the death of his Son, much more surely, having been reconciled, will we be saved by his life. But more than that, we even boast in God through our Lord Jesus Christ, through whom we have now received reconciliation.

Intercessions: We pray this day
—that God's spirit will give comfort and hope to those who suffer.
—for peace among the nations, especially for peace in_____.

43

WEEK II — Tuesday

Reconciliation with Neighbor

Opening Prayer: Source of goodness who remembers not our sins, open our lips this day to speak your praise! We give thanks that you are the hope of all the earth, the one for whom we yearn and yet from whom we so often turn away. We confess that we live possessive lives as if all we have were not a gift from you. We confess that we live prideful lives as if we were the center of creation. We confess that we live diminished lives, jealous and resentful, as if we were not enriched by another's joy. Forgive us, Lord. Ground our lives in your perfect love that never ends. We pray it in the name of him by whom we know love, Christ our Lord. Amen.

Reading from the Psalms   Psalm 51:1-17

Refrain: Have mercy on me, O God, according to your steadfast love.

Have mercy on me, O God,
    according to your steadfast love;
according to your abundant mercy
    blot out my transgressions.
Wash me thoroughly from my iniquity,
    and cleanse me from my sin.

For I know my transgressions,
    and my sin is ever before me.
Against you, you alone, have I sinned,
    and done what is evil in your sight,
so that you are justified in your sentence
    and blameless when you pass judgment.
Indeed, I was born guilty,
    a sinner when my mother conceived me.*

You desire truth in the inward being;
    therefore teach me wisdom in my secret heart.
Purge me with hyssop, and I shall be clean;
    wash me, and I shall be whiter than snow.
Let me hear joy and gladness;
    let the bones that you have crushed rejoice.

Hide your face from my sins,
    and blot out all my iniquities.*

Create in me a clean heart, O God,
    and put a new and right spirit within me.
Do not cast me away from your presence,
    and do not take your holy spirit from me.
Restore to me the joy of your salvation,
    and sustain in me a willing spirit.

Then I will teach transgressors your ways,
    and sinners will return to you.
Deliver me from bloodshed, O God,
    O God of my salvation,
    and my tongue will sing aloud of your deliverance.*

O Lord, open my lips,
    and my mouth will declare your praise.
For you have no delight in sacrifice;
    if I were to give a burnt offering, you would not be
        pleased.
The sacrifice acceptable to God is a broken spirit;
    a broken and contrite heart, O God, you will not
        despise.

Reading from the New Testament   1 Corinthians 13:1-13

If I speak in the tongues of mortals and of angels, but do not
have love, I am a noisy gong or a clanging cymbal. And if I have
prophetic powers, and understand all mysteries and all knowledge, and if I have all faith, so as to remove mountains, but do not
have love, I am nothing. If I give away all my possessions, and if
I hand over my body so that I may boast, but do not have love, I gain
nothing.
    Love is patient; love is kind; love is not envious or boastful or
arrogant or rude. It does not insist on its own way; it is not irritable
or resentful; it does not rejoice in wrongdoing, but rejoices in the
truth. It bears all things, believes all things, hopes all things,
endures all things.
    Love never ends. But as for prophecies, they will come to an
end; as for tongues, they will cease; as for knowledge, it will come
to an end. For we know only in part, and we prophesy only in part;
but when the complete comes, the partial will come to an end.
When I was a child, I spoke like a child, I thought like a child, I

reasoned like a child; when I became an adult, I put an end to childish ways. For now we see in a mirror, dimly, but then we will see face to face. Now I know only in part; then I will know fully, even as I have been fully known. And now faith, hope, and love abide, these three; and the greatest of these is love.

Intercessions: We pray this day
—that the patience and kindness of God's love will mark our lives.
—for those who suffer because of divisions in the human community, especially those in _____.

WEEK II — Wednesday

Reconciliation Within the Church

Opening Prayer: Loving God, when we pause to acknowledge the blessings that greet us each new day, truly we must stand in awe of your goodness! For the beauty and bounty of nature, for the gifts of love and compassion that bind your children together, for the gift of your church in which there is neither Jew nor Greek, black nor white, male nor female, for the promise of forgiveness and newness of life, for the example and sacrifice of Jesus in whose name we are called to serve — for all these things, we give you thanks and praise. May our lives be so filled with gratitude that we become witnesses to your grace. Amen.

Reading from the Psalms   Psalm 65

Refrain: You are the hope of all the ends of the earth.

> Praise is due to you,
>   O God, in Zion;
> and to you shall vows be performed,
>   O you who answer prayer!
> To you all flesh shall come.
> When deeds of iniquity overwhelm us,
>   you forgive our transgressions.
> Happy are those whom you choose and bring near
>   to live in your courts.

We shall be satisfied with the goodness of your house,
   your holy temple.*

By awesome deeds you answer us with deliverance,
   O God of our salvation;
you are the hope of all the ends of the earth
   and of the farthest seas.
By your strength you established the mountains;
   you are girded with might.
You silence the roaring of the seas,
   the roaring of their waves,
   the tumult of the peoples.
Those who live at earth's farthest bounds are awed by
      your signs;
you make the gateways of the morning and the evening
      shout for joy.*

You visit the earth and water it,
   you greatly enrich it;
the river of God is full of water;
   you provide the people with grain,
   for so you have prepared it.
You water its furrows abundantly,
   settling its ridges,
softening it with showers,
   and blessing its growth.
You crown the year with your bounty;
   your wagon tracks overflow with richness.
The pastures of the wilderness overflow,
   the hills gird themselves with joy,
the meadows clothe themselves with flocks,
   the valleys deck themselves with grain,
   they shout and sing together for joy.*

Reading from the New Testament   Colossians 3:9-17

Do not lie to to one another, seeing that you have stripped off
the old self with its practices and have clothed yourselves with the
new self, which is being renewed in knowledge according to the
image of its creator. In that renewal there is no longer Greek and
Jew, circumcised and uncircumcised, barbarian, Scythian, slave
and free; but Christ is all and in all!
As God's chosen ones, holy and beloved, clothe yourselves
with compassion, kindness, humility, meekness, and patience.

47

Bear with one another and, if anyone has a complaint against another, forgive each other; just as the Lord has forgiven you, so you also must forgive. Above all, clothe yourselves with love, which binds everything together in perfect harmony. And let the peace of Christ rule in your hearts, to which indeed you were called in the one body. And be thankful. Let the word of Christ dwell in you richly; teach and admonish one another in all wisdom; and with gratitude in your hearts sing psalms, hymns, and spiritual songs to God. And whatever you do, in word or deed, do everything in the name of the Lord Jesus, giving thanks to God the Father through him.

Intercessions: We pray this day
  —for the unity of the church, that our congregations may be infused with the spirit of Colossians.
  —for those facing a harvest that is not abundant, for whom nature is more menace than friend, especially those in _____.

Week II —Thursday

Reconciliation with God

Opening Prayer: Divine Parent, we rejoice to put our trust in you! With the sparrow and swallow, we find in you our home and strength. Forgive us when we desire to live with other gods, choosing bondage to things of this world and graven images of our making, rather than yearning for a day in your courts. Again and again — at Sinai, at Calvary, in our daily lives — you call us back to our true dwelling place. Enable us, we pray, to hear that call. Through Christ our Lord. Amen.

Reading from the Psalms   Psalm 84

Refrain: Happy are those who live in your house, ever singing your praise.

How lovely is your dwelling place,
  O LORD of hosts!

My soul longs, indeed it faints
for the courts of the LORD;
my heart and my flesh sing for joy
to the living God.*

Even the sparrow finds a home,
and the swallow a nest for herself,
where she may lay her young,
at your altars, O LORD of hosts,
my King and my God.
Happy are those who live in your house,
ever singing your praise.

Happy are those whose strength is in you,
in whose heart are the highways to Zion.
As they go through the valley of Baca
they make it a place of springs;
the early rain also covers it with pools.
They go from strength to strength;
the God of gods will be seen in Zion.*

O LORD God of hosts, hear my prayer;
give ear, O God of Jacob!
Behold our shield, O God;
look on the face of your anointed.

For a day in your courts is better
than a thousand elsewhere.
I would rather be a doorkeeper in the house of my God
than live in the tents of wickedness.
For the LORD God is a sun and shield;
he bestows favor and honor.
No good thing does the LORD withhold
from those who walk uprightly.
O LORD of hosts,
happy is everyone who trusts in you.*

Reading from the New Testament   Galatians 4:1-9

My point is this: heirs, as long as they are minors, are no better
than slaves, though they are the owners of all the property; but they
remain under guardians and trustees until the date set by the
father. So with us; while we were minors, we were enslaved to the
elemental spirits of the world. But when the fullness of time had

49

come, God sent his Son, born of a woman, born under the law, in order to redeem those who were under the law, so that we might receive adoption as children. And because you are children, God has sent the Spirit of his Son into our hearts, crying "Abba! Father!" So you are no longer a slave but a child, and if a child then also an heir, through God.

Formerly, when you did not know God, you were enslaved to beings that by nature are not gods. Now, however, that you have come to know God, or rather to be known by God, how can you turn back again to the weak and beggarly elemental spirits? How can you want to be enslaved to them again?

Intercessions: We pray this day
—for those who measure their lives by the accumulation of wealth or power.
—for the homeless and all who care for them, especially the homeless in _____ .

WEEK II — Friday

Reconciliation with Neighbor

Opening Prayer: God of steadfast love and faithfulness, source of life in all its fullness, we join our voices with the generations who have sung your praise. We give thanks for the covenant you made with our ancestor David, and for the covenant extended to us through Jesus Christ. We give thanks that as you forgave our ancestors, so you forgive us far beyond all deserving. Yet we who yearn for forgiveness often fail to extend it to others. Chasten us, Lord. Help us to see your image in the faces of those we encounter this day. Amen.

Reading from the Psalms   Psalm 89:1-16

Refrain: I will sing of your steadfast love, O Lord, forever.

I will sing of your steadfast love, O LORD, forever;
   with my mouth I will proclaim your faithfulness to all
      generations.

50

I declare that your steadfast love is established forever;
   your faithfulness is as firm as the heavens.

You said, "I have made a covenant with my chosen
      one,
   I have sworn to my servant David:
'I will establish your descendants forever,
   and build your throne for all generations.'"*

Let the heavens praise your wonders, O LORD,
   your faithfulness in the assembly of the holy ones.
For who in the skies can be compared to the LORD?
   Who among the heavenly beings is like the LORD,
a God feared in the council of the holy ones,
   great and awesome above all that are around him?
O LORD God of hosts,
   who is as mighty as you, O LORD?
   Your faithfulness surrounds you.*
You rule the raging of the sea;
   when its waves rise, you still them.
You crushed Rahab like a carcass;
   you scattered your enemies with your mighty arm.
The heavens are yours, the earth also is yours;
   the world and all that is in it — you have founded
      them.
The north and the south — you created them;
   Tabor and Hermon joyously praise your name.*
You have a mighty arm;
   strong is your hand, high your right hand.
Righteousness and justice are the foundation of your
      throne;
   steadfast love and faithfulness go before you.
Happy are the people who know the festal shout,
   who walk, O LORD, in the light of your countenance;
they exult in your name all day long,
   and extol your righteousness.*

Reading from the New Testament   Matthew 18:21-35

Then Peter came and said to him, "Lord, if another member of
the church sins against me, how often should I forgive? As many as
seven times?" Jesus said to him, "Not seven times, but, I tell you,
seventy-seven times.

51

"For this reason the kingdom of heaven may be compared to a king who wished to settle accounts with his slaves. When he began the reckoning, one who owed him ten thousand talents was brought to him; and, as he could not pay, his lord ordered him to be sold, together with his wife and children and all his possessions, and payment to be made. So the slave fell on his knees before him, saying, 'Have patience with me, and I will pay you everything.' And out of pity for him, the lord of that slave released him and forgave him the debt. But that same slave, as he went out, came upon one of his fellow slaves who owed him a hundred denarii; and seizing him by the throat, he said, 'Pay what you owe.' Then his fellow slave fell down and pleaded with him, 'Have patience with me, and I will pay you.' But he refused; then he went and threw him into prison until he would pay the debt. When his fellow slaves saw what had happened, they were greatly distressed, and they went and reported to their lord all that had taken place. Then his lord summoned him and said to him, 'You wicked slave! I forgave you all that debt because you pleaded with me. Should you not have had mercy on your fellow slave, as I had mercy on you?' And in anger his lord handed him over to be tortured until he would pay his entire debt. So my heavenly Father will also do to every one of you, if you do not forgive your brother or sister from your heart."

Intercessions: We pray this day
—for those we have not forgiven and for those who have not forgiven us.
—for places around the world where hatred and suspicion obscure the presence of God, especially _____.

WEEK II—Saturday

Reconciliation Within the Church

Opening Prayer: Dear God, source and center of our lives, we begin this day by declaring your marvelous works! We give thanks for the diversity of people you have created — people of different colors and cultures, of different languages and nations. We give thanks for the church in which, by your Spirit, our diversity is forged into a family of mutual care. We give thanks for the gift of Jesus Christ through whom we have come to know you and to know ourselves as loved and forgiven. Loving and forgiving God, we have no worthy gifts to set before you except our lives, which we offer this day to your glory. Amen.

Reading from the Psalms   Psalm 96

Refrain: Great is the Lord, and greatly to be praised.

O sing to the LORD a new song;
    sing to the LORD, all the earth.
Sing to the LORD, bless his name;
    tell of his salvation from day to day.
Declare his glory among the nations,
    his marvelous works among all the peoples.
For great is the LORD, and greatly to be praised;
    he is to be revered above all gods.
For all the gods of the peoples are idols,
    but the LORD made the heavens.
Honor and majesty are before him;
    strength and beauty are in his sanctuary.*

Ascribe to the LORD, O families of the peoples,
    ascribe to the LORD glory and strength.
Ascribe to the LORD the glory due his name;
    bring an offering, and come into his courts.
Worship the LORD in holy splendor;
    tremble before him, all the earth.*

Say among the nations, "The LORD is king!
    The world is firmly established; it shall never be
        moved.
    He will judge the peoples with equity."
Let the heavens be glad, and let the earth rejoice;
    let the sea roar, and all that fills it;
    let the field exult, and everything in it.
Then shall all the trees of the forest sing for joy
    before the LORD; for he is coming,
    for he is coming to judge the earth.
He will judge the people with righteousness,
    and the peoples with his truth.

Reading from the New Testament 1 Corinthians 12:12-26

For just as the body is one and has many members, and all the members of the body, though many, are one body, so it is with Christ. For in the one Spirit we were all baptized into one body—Jews or Greeks, slaves or free—and we were all made to drink of one Spirit.

Indeed, the body does not consist of one member but of many. If the foot would say, "Because I am not a hand, I do not belong to the body," that would not make it any less a part of the body. And if the ear would say, "Because I am not an eye, I do not belong to the body," that would not make it any less a part of the body. If the whole body were an eye, where would the hearing be? If the whole body were hearing, where would the sense of smell be? But as it is, God arranged the members in the body, each one of them, as he chose. If all were a single member, where would the body be? As it is, there are many members, yet one body. The eye cannot say to the hand, "I have no need of you," nor again the head to the feet, "I have no need of you." On the contrary, the members of the body that seem to be weaker are indispensable, and those members of the body that we think less honorable we clothe with greater honor, and our less respectable members are treated with greater respect; whereas our more respectable members do not need this. But God has so arranged the body, giving the greater honor to the inferior member, that there may be no dissension within the body, but the members may have the same care for one another. If one member suffers, all suffer together with it; if one member is honored, all rejoice together with it.

Intercessions: We pray this day
    —for the church in every place, especially the church in _____.
    —that God may enable the church to be a place where the world's diversity is welcome.

WEEK II — Sunday

The Lord's Supper

Opening Prayer: O source of truth and righteousness, you are God and greatly to be praised! We give thanks for the vision of the day when the earth shall be as full of the knowledge of the Lord as waters covering the sea. We know deep within us both the truth of this vision and the unholy way in which we live. Forgive us, holy Creator, for the times we deny your sovereignty. Draw us nearer to you through the sacrifice of your Son, whose body and blood we share. Inspire us, through your Spirit, to stir up one another to love. Amen.

Reading from the Prophets   Isaiah 11:1-9

A shoot shall come out from the stump of Jesse,
and a branch shall grow out of his roots.
The spirit of the LORD shall rest on him,
    the spirit of wisdom and understanding,
    the spirit of counsel and might,
    the spirit of knowledge and the fear of the LORD.
His delight shall be in the fear of the LORD.

He shall not judge by what his eyes see,
    or decide by what his ears hear;
but with righteousness he shall judge the poor,
    and decide with equity for the meek of the earth;
he shall strike the earth with the rod of his mouth,
    and with the breath of his lips he shall kill the
        wicked.
Righteousness shall be the belt around his waist,
    and faithfulness the belt around his loins.

The wolf shall live with the lamb,
    the leopard shall lie down with the kid,
the calf and the lion and the fatling together,
    and a little child shall lead them.
The cow and the bear shall graze,
    their young shall lie down together;
    and the lion shall eat straw like the ox.
The nursing child shall play over the hole of the asp,

and the weaned child shall put its hand on the adder's
   den.
They will not hurt or destroy
   on all my holy mountain;
for the earth will be full of the knowledge of the LORD
   as the waters cover the sea.

Reading from the New Testament   Hebrews 10:11-25

And every priest stands day after day at his service, offering
again and again the same sacrifices that can never take away sins.
But when Christ had offered for all time a single sacrifice for sins,
"he sat down at the right hand of God," and since then has been
waiting "until his enemies would be made a footstool for his feet."
For by a single offering he has perfected for all time those who are
sanctified. And the Holy Spirit also testifies to us, for after saying,
   "This is the covenant that I will make with them
      after those days, says the Lord:
   I will put my laws in their hearts,
      and I will write them on their minds,"
   he also adds,
   "I will remember their sins and their lawless deeds no
      more."
Where there is forgiveness of these, there is no longer any
offering for sin.
   Therefore, my friends, since we have confidence to enter the
sanctuary by the blood of Jesus, by the new and living way that he
opened for us through the curtain (that is, through his flesh), and
since we have a great priest over the house of God, let us approach
with a true heart in full assurance of faith, with our hearts sprinkled
clean from an evil conscience and our bodies washed with pure
water. Let us hold fast to the confession of our hope without
wavering, for he who has promised is faithful. And let us consider
how to provoke one another to love and good deeds, not neglecting
to meet together, as is the habit of some, but encouraging one
another, and all the more as you see the Day approaching.

Intercessions: We pray this day
   —that the church will confess its hope in God without wavering.
   —that, as we are fed and nourished by Christ's body, so we
will seek to feed and nourish the hungry.

Reconciliation with God

Opening Prayer: Compassionate God, you are the author of life and salvation and greatly to be praised! Open our eyes this day to see ourselves as others see us and as you would have us be. Turn our minds from a love of lesser things to a deeper love for you and those, our brothers and sisters, who are your children. Strengthen our wills to hate evil and seek reconciliation, even when it is costly to do so. We pray it in the name of Christ Jesus, our Lord, who gave himself on the cross that the world might know peace. Amen.

Reading from the Psalms   Psalm 97

(The asterisks [*] indicate where the refrain may be repeated or where the psalm may be broken for antiphonal reading.)

Refrain: Light dawns for the righteous, and joy for the upright in heart.

The LORD is king! Let the earth rejoice;
    let the many coastlands be glad!
Clouds and thick darkness are all around him;
    righteousness and justice are the foundation of his throne.
Fire goes before him,
    and consumes his adversaries on every side.
His lightnings light up the world;
    the earth sees and trembles.
The mountains melt like wax before the LORD,
    before the Lord of all the earth.*

The heavens proclaim his righteousness;
    and all the peoples behold his glory.
All worshipers of images are put to shame,
    those who make their boast in worthless idols;
    all gods bow down before him.
Zion hears and is glad,
    and the towns of Judah rejoice,
    because of your judgments, O God.
For you, O LORD, are most high over all the earth;
    you are exalted far above all gods.*

The LORD loves those who hate evil;
    he guards the lives of his faithful;

he rescues them from the hand of the wicked.
Light dawns for the righteous,
    and joy for the upright in heart.
Rejoice in the LORD, O you righteous,
    and give thanks to his holy name!

Reading from the New Testament   Colossians 1:15-23a

He is the image of the invisible God, the firstborn of all creation;
for in him all things in heaven and on earth were created, things
visible and invisible, whether thrones or dominions or rulers or
powers—all things have been created through him and for him. He
himself is before all things, and in him all things hold together. He
is the head of the body, the church; he is the beginning, the firstborn
from the dead, so that he might come to have first place in
everything. For in him all the fullness of God was pleased to dwell,
and through him God was pleased to reconcile to himself all things,
whether on earth or in heaven, by making peace through the blood
of his cross.

And you who were once estranged and hostile in mind, doing
evil deeds, he has now reconciled in his fleshly body through death,
so as to present you holy and blameless and irreproachable before
him—provided that you continue securely established and steadfast in the faith, without shifting from the hope promised by the
gospel that you heard, which has been proclaimed to every crea-
ture under heaven.

Intercessions: We pray this day
    —for those who have given their allegiance to the powers of
    this world.
    —for new Christians at the beginning of their journey of faith.

WEEK III—Tuesday

Reconciliation with Neighbor

Opening Prayer: Creator God, who gives us the day's length and
the night's rest, we praise your holy name! With sisters and
brothers from all the ends of the earth, we give thanks for your just

and faithful love that fills our lives. We who would be your people pray for goodness in our living, that we may learn to hate what is evil and hold fast to what is good. We pray for a new song that we can sing with our neighbors, filling the earth with psalms to glorify all your deeds. Keep us safe this day, O God, and bring us to you at its close. Amen.

Reading from the Psalms   Psalm 98

Refrain: Make a joyful noise to the Lord, all the earth.

O sing to the LORD a new song,
    for he has done marvelous things.
His right hand and his holy arm
    have gotten him victory.
The LORD has made known his victory;
    he has revealed his vindication in the sight of the nations.
He has remembered his steadfast love and faithfulness
    to the house of Israel.
All the ends of the earth have seen
    the victory of our God.

Make a joyful noise to the LORD, all the earth;
    break forth into joyous song and sing praises.
Sing praises to the LORD with the lyre,
    with the lyre and the sound of melody.
With trumpets and the sound of the horn
    make a joyful noise before the King, the LORD.*

Let the sea roar, and all that fills it;
    the world and those who live in it.
Let the floods clap their hands;
    let the hills sing together for joy
at the presence of the LORD, for he is coming
    to judge the earth.
He will judge the world with righteousness,
    and the peoples with equity.*

Reading from the New Testament   Romans 12:9-21

Let love be genuine; hate what is evil, hold fast to what is good; love one another with mutual affection; outdo one another in showing honor. Do not lag in zeal, be ardent in spirit, serve the Lord. Rejoice in hope, be patient in suffering, persevere in prayer.

Contribute to the needs of the saints; extend hospitality to strangers.

Bless those who persecute you; bless and do not curse them. Rejoice with those who rejoice, weep with those who weep. Live in harmony with one another; do not be haughty, but associate with the lowly; do not claim to be wiser than you are. Do not repay anyone evil for evil, but take thought for what is noble in the sight of all. If it is possible, so far as it depends on you, live peaceably with all. Beloved, never avenge yourselves, but leave room for the wrath of God; for it is written, "Vengeance is mine, I will repay, says the Lord." No, "if your enemies are hungry, feed them; if they are thirsty, give them something to drink; for by doing this you will heap burning coals on their heads." Do not be overcome by evil, but overcome evil with good.

Intercessions: We pray this day
—for places caught up in cycles of retribution.
—that the church might be a sign of patience, harmony, and hope.

WEEK III—Wednesday

Reconciliation Within the Church

Opening Prayer: God of faithful love, who takes the side of the oppressed and whose mercy takes away our sins, we praise you for your greatness and we give thanks for your goodness! When during this day we are impatient with our neighbors, strengthen us, O God. When during this day we are jealous of their various gifts or boastful of our own, admonish us, O God. When during this day we forget to speak the truth in love as members of a single body, challenge us, O God. When during this day we place our trust in the idols of this world, save us, O God, and turn us back to your holy will. Through Christ we pray. Amen.

Reading from the Psalms   Psalm 103:1-18

Refrain: Let all that is within me, bless God's holy name.

Bless the LORD, O my soul,
    and all that is within me,
    bless his holy name.
Bless the LORD, O my soul,
    and do not forget all his benefits—
who forgives all your iniquity,
    who heals all your diseases,
who redeems your life from the Pit,
    who crowns you with steadfast love and mercy,
who satisfies you with good as long as you live
    so that your youth is renewed like the eagle's.*

The LORD works vindication
    and justice for all who are oppressed.
He made known his ways to Moses,
    his acts to the people of Israel.
The LORD is merciful and gracious,
    slow to anger and abounding in steadfast love.
He will not always accuse,
    nor will he keep his anger forever.
He does not deal with us according to our sins,
    nor repay us according to our iniquities.
For as the heavens are high above the earth,
    so great is his steadfast love toward those who fear him;
As far as the east is from the west,
    so far he removes our transgressions from us.
As a father has compassion for his children,
    so the LORD has compassion for those who fear him.
For he knows how we were made;
    he remembers that we are dust.*

As for mortals, their days are like grass;
    they flourish like a flower of the field;
for the wind passes over it, and it is gone,
    and its place knows it no more.
But the steadfast love of the LORD is from everlasting to
       everlasting
    on those who fear him,
    and his righteousness to children's children,
to those who keep his covenant
    and remember to do his commandments.

61

Reading from the New Testament Ephesians 4:1-7, 11-16

I therefore, the prisoner in the Lord, beg you to lead a life worthy of the calling to which you have been called, with all humility and gentleness, with patience, bearing with one another in love, making every effort to maintain the unity of the Spirit in the bond of peace. There is one body and one Spirit, just as you were called to the one hope of your calling, one Lord, one faith, one baptism, one God and Father of all, who is above all and through all and in all.

But each of us was given grace according to the measure of Christ's gift.

The gifts he gave were that some would be apostles, some prophets, some evangelists, some pastors and teachers, to equip the saints for the work of ministry, for building up the body of Christ, until all of us come to the unity of the faith and of the knowledge of the Son of God, to maturity, to the measure of the full stature of Christ. We must no longer be children, tossed to and from and blown about by every wind of doctrine, by people's trickery, by their craftiness in deceitful scheming. But speaking the truth in love, we must grow up in every way into him who is the head, into Christ, from whom the whole body, joined and knit together by every ligament with which it is equipped, as each part is working properly, promotes the body's growth in building itself up in love.

Intercessions: We pray this day
—for unity and maturity of faith in our congregations.
—that the members of our congregations will learn to use the gifts of ministry with which they have been blessed.

WEEK III—Thursday

Reconciliation with God

Opening Prayer: O source of life, whose power it is to send the sun and moon spinning on their course that we might know our life's passage and the seasons of the earth, we stand at this day's threshold and wonder that we are part of your creation. How great

you are, O God! You have provided everything we need: the planet
on which we live, daily bread that makes us strong, strangers and
friends with whom we grow, the living water of your Son, Jesus
Christ, which quenches our thirst forever. It is in his name we pray.
Amen.

Reading from the Psalms   Psalm 104:1-15

Refrain: Bless the Lord, O my soul.

Bless the LORD, O my soul.
> O LORD my God, you are very great.
You are clothed with honor and majesty,
> wrapped in light as with a garment.
You stretch out the heavens like a tent,
> you set the beams of your chambers on the waters,
you make the clouds your chariot,
> you ride on the wings of the wind,
you make the winds your messengers,
> fire and flame your ministers.*

You set the earth on its foundations,
> so that it shall never be shaken.
You cover it with the deep as with a garment;
> the waters stood above the mountains.
At your rebuke they flee;
> at the sound of your thunder they take to flight.
They rose up to the mountains, ran down to the valleys
> to the place that you appointed for them.
You set a boundary that they may not pass,
> so that they might not again cover the earth.*

You make springs gush forth in the valleys;
> they flow between the hills,
giving drink to every wild animal;
> the wild asses quench their thirst.
By the streams the birds of the air have their habitation;
> they sing among the branches.
From your lofty abode you water the mountains;
> the earth is satisfied with the fruit of your work.*

You cause the grass to grow for the cattle,
> and plants for people to use,
to bring forth food from the earth,
> and wine to gladden the human heart,

oil to make the face shine,
and bread to strengthen the human heart.

Reading from the New Testament   John 4:7-15

A Samaritan woman came to draw water, and Jesus said to her, "Give me a drink." (His disciples had gone to the city to buy food.) The Samaritan woman said to him, "How is it that you, a Jew, ask a drink of me, a woman of Samaria?" (Jews do not share things in common with Samaritans.) Jesus answered her, "If you knew the gift of God, and who it is that is saying to you, 'Give me a drink,' you would have asked him, and he would have given you living water." The woman said to him, "Sir, you have no bucket, and the well is deep. Where do you get that living water? Are you greater than our ancestor Jacob, who gave us the well, and with his sons and his flocks drank from it?" Jesus said to her, "Everyone who drinks of this water will be thirsty again, but those who drink of the water that I will give them will never be thirsty. The water that I will give will become in them a spring of water gushing up to eternal life." The woman said to him, "Sir, give me this water, so that I may never be thirsty or have to keep coming here to draw water."

Intercessions: We pray this day
—that humankind will learn to love creation, not just use it.
—that our communities may be open to hear God's call from unexpected sources.

WEEK III—Friday

Reconciliation with Neighbor

Opening Prayer: O wondrous love, by your spirit we are created, by your spirit we are sustained, by your spirit we and the world are made new. If you turn your face away, we suffer. If you stop our breath, we die and return to dust. Help us to live in the knowledge of our dependence on your mighty hand. Turn us from the pride and self-centeredness that blind us to your will and to our neighbors' needs. Enable us to be constant in our call, praising your name and teaching your word, that when evening falls our lives will be found pleasing to you. Amen.

Reading from the Psalms   Psalm 104:24-35

Refrain: May the glory of the Lord endure forever.

O LORD, how manifold are your works!
    In wisdom you have made them all;
    the earth is full of your creatures.
Yonder is the sea, great and wide,
    creeping things innumerable are there,
    living things both small and great.
There go the ships,
    and Leviathan that you formed to sport in it.*

These all look to you
    to give them their food in due season;
when you give to them, they gather it up;
    when you open your hand, they are filled with good
        things.
When you hide your face, they are dismayed;
    when you take away their breath they die
    and return to their dust.
When you send forth your spirit, they are created;
    and you renew the face of the ground.*

May the glory of the LORD endure forever;
    may the LORD rejoice in his works—
who looks on the earth and it trembles,
    who touches the mountains and they smoke.
I will sing to the LORD as long as I live;
    I will sing praise to my God while I have being.
May my meditation be pleasing to him,
    for I rejoice in the LORD.
Let sinners be consumed from the earth,
    and let the wicked be no more.
Bless the LORD, O my soul.
Praise the LORD!

Reading from the New Testament   2 Timothy 3:14—4:5

But as for you, continue in what you have learned and firmly
believed, knowing from whom you learned it, and how from
childhood you have known the sacred writings that are able to
instruct you for salvation through faith in Christ Jesus. All scrip-

ture is inspired by God and is useful for teaching, for reproof, for correction, and for training in righteousness, so that everyone who belongs to God may be proficient, equipped for every good work.

In the presence of God and of Christ Jesus, who is to judge the living and the dead, and in view of his appearing and his kingdom, I solemnly urge you: proclaim the message; be persistent whether the time is favorable or unfavorable; convince, rebuke, and encourage, with the utmost patience in teaching. For the time is coming when people will not put up with sound doctrine, but having itching ears, they will accumulate for themselves teachers to suit their own desires, and will turn away from listening to the truth and wander away to myths. As for you, always be sober, endure suffering, do the work of an evangelist, carry out your ministry fully.

Intercessions: We pray this day
—for the poor who are often denied the fruits of God's creation.
—for those who labor to preserve the balance of nature.

WEEK III—Saturday

Reconciliation Within the Church

Opening Prayer: Blessed are you, O Lord our God, ruler of the universe! You have offered us the holy word of your commandments, and we give you thanks. You have shown us your nature and purpose in Jesus Christ, and we give you thanks. You have called us into a single community of faith as a sign to the world, and we give you thanks. Lead us this day where you would have us go and preserve us, we pray, from all harm. In Christ's name. Amen.

Reading from the Psalms   Psalm 119:1-16

Refrain: Happy are those whose way is blameless, who walk in the law of the Lord.

Happy are those whose way is blameless,
    who walk in the law of the LORD.

Happy are those who keep his decrees,
　　who seek him with their whole heart,
who also do no wrong,
　　but walk in his ways.
You have commanded your precepts
　　to be kept diligently.
O that my ways may be steadfast
　　in keeping your statutes!
Then I shall not be put to shame,
　　having my eyes fixed on all your commandments.
I will praise you with an upright heart,
　　when I learn your righteous ordinances.
I will observe your statutes;
　　do not utterly forsake me.*

How can young people keep their way pure?
　　By guarding it according to your word.
With my whole heart I seek you;
　　do not let me stray from your commandments.
I treasure your word in my heart,
　　so that I may not sin against you.
Blessed are you, O LORD;
　　teach me your statutes.
With my lips I declare
　　all the ordinances of your mouth.
I delight in the way of your decrees
　　as much as in all riches.
I will meditate on your precepts,
　　and fix my eyes on your ways.
I will delight in your statutes;
　　I will not forget your word.*

Reading from the New Testament　　　　John 17:20-26

　　"I ask not only on behalf of these, but also on behalf of those who will believe in me through their word, that they may all be one. As you, Father, are in me and I am in you, may they also be in us, so that the world may believe that you have sent me. The glory that you have given me I have given them, so that they may be one, as we are one, I in them and you in me, that they may become completely one, so that the world may know that you have sent me and have loved them even as you have loved me. Father, I desire that those also, whom you have given me, may be with me where I am, to see my glory, which you have given me because you loved me before the foundation of the world.

"Righteous Father, the world does not know you, but I know you; and these know that you have sent me. I made your name known to them, and I will make it known, so that the love with which you have loved me may be in them, and I in them."

Intercessions: We pray this day
—for the reconciliation of "evangelical Christians" and "ecumenical Christians."
—that the church may be a faithful witness to the unity God intends for the world.

WEEK III—Sunday

The Lord's Supper

Opening Prayer: Hear our prayer, O God. On this day when we come together for worship, hear our prayer. We thank you for your word—proclaimed by the prophets, embodied in Jesus Christ—through which we know your divine purpose. But we confess that we have betrayed this living word. We thank you for the vision of your reign when all persons shall live in joy and peace. But we confess that we have ignored this vision. We thank you for the fellowship of your church, a community of all races and nations, which breaks one loaf and drinks from one cup. But we confess that we have denied this unity. Forgive us, loving Parent, and lift our thoughts to you. Through Christ our Lord we pray. Amen.

Reading from the Prophets   Isaiah 55:6-13

Seek the LORD while he may be found,
    call upon him while he is near;
let the wicked forsake their way,
    and the unrighteous their thoughts;
let them return to the LORD, that he may have mercy on them,
    and to our God, for he will abundantly pardon.
For my thoughts are not your thoughts,
    nor are your ways my ways, says the LORD.

68

For as the heavens are higher than the earth,
 so are my ways higher than your ways
 and my thoughts than your thoughts.

For as the rain and snow come down from heaven,
 and do not return there until they have watered the
  earth,
making it bring forth and sprout,
 giving seed to the sower and bread to the eater,
so shall my word be that goes out from my mouth;
 it shall not return to me empty,
but it shall accomplish that which I purpose,
 and succeed in the thing for which I sent it.

For you shall go out in joy,
 and be led back in peace;
the mountains and the hills before you
 shall burst into song,
 and all the trees of the field shall clap their hands.
Instead of the thorn shall come up the cypress;
 instead of the brier shall come up the myrtle;
and it shall be to the LORD for a memorial,
 for an everlasting sign that shall not be cut off.

Reading from the New Testament   Matthew 26:17-29

On the first day of Unleavened Bread the disciples came to Jesus, saying, "Where do you want us to make the preparations for you to eat the Passover?" He said, "Go into the city to a certain man, and say to him, 'The Teacher says, My time is near; I will keep the Passover at your house with my disciples.'" So the disciples did as Jesus had directed them, and they prepared the Passover meal.

When it was evening, he took his place with the twelve; and while they were eating, he said, "Truly I tell you, one of you will betray me." And they became greatly distressed and began to say to him one after another, "Surely not I, Lord?" He answered, "The one who has dipped his hand into the bowl with me will betray me. The Son of Man goes as it is written of him, but woe to that one by whom the Son of Man is betrayed! It would have been better for that one not to have been born." Judas, who betrayed him, said, "Surely not I, Rabbi?" He replied, "You have said so."

While they were eating, Jesus took a loaf of bread, and after blessing it he broke it, gave it to the disciples, and said, "Take, eat; this is my body." Then he took a cup, and after giving thanks he gave it to them, saying, "Drink from it, all of you; for this is my blood of the covenant, which is poured out for many for the forgiveness of sins. I tell you, I will never again drink of this fruit of the vine until that day when I drink it new with you in my Father's kingdom."

Intercessions: We pray this day
  —for those for whom faith in God is not easy.
  —that the church may become the body of Christ, broken and given for the world.

WEEK IV—Monday

Reconciliation with God

Opening Prayer: Guardian and Comforter, without you we are nothing. We are lost sheep in need of a shepherd to lead and care for us. But you have not abandoned us! We give thanks that you keep us from evil and protect us through the night. We rejoice that you have given us all we need, especially your Son, Jesus Christ. Therefore, we pray with jubilant voices. For through Christ, we have the assurance that nothing separates us from your love. Amen.

Reading from the Psalms   Psalm 121

(The asterisks [*] indicate where the refrain may be repeated or where the psalm may be broken for antiphonal reading.)

Refrain: My help comes from the Lord, who made heaven and earth.

I lift up my eyes to the hills—
    from where will my help come?
My help comes from the LORD,
    who made heaven and earth.

He will not let your foot be moved;
    he who keeps you will not slumber.
He who keeps Israel
    will neither slumber nor sleep.

The LORD is your keeper;
    the LORD is your shade at your right hand.
The sun shall not strike you by day,
    nor the moon by night.

The LORD will keep you from all evil;
    he will keep your life.
The LORD will keep
    your going out and your coming in
    from this time on and forevermore.*

Reading from the New Testament   Romans 8:31-39

What then are we to say about these things? If God is for us, who is against us? He who did not withhold his own Son, but gave him up for all of us, will he not with him also give us everything else? Who will bring any charge against God's elect? It is God who justifies. Who is to condemn? It is Christ Jesus, who died, yes, who was raised, who is at the right hand of God, who indeed intercedes for us. Who will separate us from the love of Christ? Will hardship, or distress, or persecution, or famine, or nakedness, or peril, or sword? As it is written,
  "For your sake we are being killed all day long;
    we are accounted as sheep to be slaughtered."
No, in all these things we are more than conquerors through him who loved us. For I am convinced that neither death, nor life, nor angels, nor rulers, nor things present, nor things to come, nor powers, nor height, nor depth, nor anything else in all creation, will be able to separate us from the love of God in Christ Jesus our Lord.

Intercessions: We pray this day
  —for those who risk their lives in proclaiming God's love.
  —for families that are separated, unable to care for one another.

WEEK IV—Tuesday

Reconciliation with Neighbor

Opening Prayer: Creator God, who formed us in the womb and numbered our days before they began, how boundless is your knowledge and your love! We thank you for the countless ways you come to us, especially in the gift of Jesus Christ, our Lord. In him, we are called to a perfect love that casts out fear and makes us new. In him, we are called to a universal love that binds us in one family with women and men of every culture and race. Fill us anew with this spirit of Christ! Hold us up to your powerful wind that what is chaff in us may be blown away and what is truly of your making may remain to guide us. Amen.

Reading from the Psalms

Psalm 139:1-15, 23-24

Refrain: Search me, O God, and know my heart; test me and know my thoughts.

O LORD, you have searched me and known me.
You know when I sit down and when I rise up;
    you discern my thoughts from far away.
You search out my path and my lying down,
    and are acquainted with all my ways.
Even before a word is on my tongue,
    O LORD, you know it completely.
You hem me in, behind and before,
    and lay your hand upon me.
Such knowledge is too wonderful for me;
    it is so high that I cannot attain it.*

Where can I go from your spirit?
    Or where can I flee from your presence?
If I ascend to heaven, you are there;
        if I make my bed in Sheol, you are there.
If I take the wings of the morning
    and settle at the farthest limits of the sea,
even there your hand shall lead me,
    and your right hand shall hold me fast.
If I say, "Surely the darkness shall cover me,
    and the light around me become night,"
even the darkness is not dark to you;
    the night is as bright as the day,
    for darkness is as light to you.*

For it was you who formed my inward parts;
    you knit me together in my mother's womb.
I praise you, for I am fearfully and wonderfully made.
    Wonderful are your works;
    that I know very well.
    My frame was not hidden from you,
when I was being made in secret,
    intricately woven in the depths of the earth.

Search me, O God, and know my heart;
    test me and know my thoughts.
See if there is any wicked way in me,
    and lead me in the way everlasting.

Beloved, let us love one another, because love is from God; everyone who loves is born of God and knows God. Whoever does not love does not know God, for God is love. God's love was revealed among us in this way; God sent his only Son into the world so that we might live through him. In this is love, not that we loved God but that he loved us and sent his Son to be the atoning sacrifice for our sins. Beloved, since God loved us so much, we also ought to love one another. No one has ever seen God; if we love one another, God lives in us, and his love is perfected in us.

By this we know that we abide in him and he in us, because he has given us of his Spirit. And we have seen and do testify that the Father has sent his Son as the Savior of the world. God abides in those who confess that Jesus is the Son of God, and they abide in God. So we have known and believe the love that God has for us.

God is love, and those who abide in love abide in God, and God abides in them. Love has been perfected among us in this: that we may have boldness on the day of judgment, because as he is, so are we in this world. There is no fear in love, but perfect love casts out fear; for fear has to do with punishment, and whoever fears has not reached perfection in love. We love because he first loved us. Those who say, "I love God" and hate their brothers or sisters, are liars; for those who do not love a brother or sister whom they have seen, cannot love God whom they have not seen. The commandment we have from him is this: those who love God must love their brothers and sisters also.

Intercessions: We pray this day
—for those who suffer from the absence of love, especially children without parents and the elderly without family.
—for those who foster the sin of racial hatred and those who suffer at their hand.

WEEK IV—Wednesday

Reconciliation Within the Church

Opening Prayer: Almighty God—who is without equal, whose greatness is beyond our understanding—each generation tells the next of your mercy and grace. We desire to be numbered among your faithful ones, but too often we refuse to give up childish ways. Forgive us when we sow strife and jealousy. Forgive us when we proclaim ourselves rather than you. You alone give the growth; you alone lift up the fallen; you alone sent your Son in whom we are bound as one body. In his name we pray. Amen.

Reading from the Psalms   Psalm 145:1-16, 21

Refrain: Every day we will bless you, and praise your name forever and ever.

I will extol you, my God and King,
   and bless your name forever and ever.
Every day I will bless you,
   and praise your name forever and ever.
Great is the LORD, and greatly to be praised;
   his greatness is unsearchable.

One generation shall laud your works to another,
   and shall declare your mighty acts.
On the glorious splendor of your majesty,
   and on your wondrous works, I will meditate.
The might of your awesome deeds shall be proclaimed,
   and I will declare your greatness.
They shall celebrate the fame of your abundant goodness,
   and shall sing aloud of your righteousness.*

The LORD is gracious and merciful,
   slow to anger and abounding in steadfast love.
The LORD is good to all,
   and his compassion is over all that he has made.

All your works shall give thanks to you, O LORD,
   and all your faithful shall bless you.
They shall speak of the glory of your kingdom,

75

and tell of your power,
to make known to all people your mighty deeds,
    and the glorious splendor of your kingdom.
Your kingdom is an everlasting kingdom,
    and your dominion endures throughout all generations.*

The LORD is faithful in all his words,
    and gracious in all his deeds.
The LORD upholds all who are falling,
    and raises up all who are bowed down.
The eyes of all look to you,
    and you give them their food in due season.
You open your hand,
    satisfying the desire of every living thing.

My mouth will speak the praise of the LORD
    and all flesh will bless his holy name forever and ever.

Reading from the New Testament
1 Corinthians 1:10-13; 3:1-9

Now I appeal to you, brothers and sisters, by the name of our Lord Jesus Christ, that all of you be in agreement and that there be no divisions among you, but that you be united in the same mind and the same purpose. For it has been reported to me by Chloe's people that there are quarrels among you, my brothers and sisters. What I mean is that each of you says, "I belong to Paul," or "I belong to Apollos" or "I belong to Cephas," or "I belong to Christ." Has Christ been divided? Was Paul crucified for you? Or were you baptized in the name of Paul?

And so, brothers and sisters, I could not speak to you as spiritual people, but rather as people of the flesh, as infants in Christ. I fed you with milk, not solid food, for you were not ready for solid food. Even now you are still not ready, for you are still of the flesh. For as long as there is jealousy and quarreling among you, are you not of the flesh, and behaving according to human inclinations? For when one says, "I belong to Paul," and another, "I belong to Apollos," are you not merely human?

What then is Apollos? What is Paul? Servants through whom you came to believe, as the Lord assigned to each. I planted, Apollos watered, but God gave the growth. So neither the one who plants nor the one who waters is anything, but only God who gives the growth. The one who plants and the one who waters have a common purpose, and each will receive wages according to the

76

labor of each. For we are God's servants, working together; you are God's field, God's building.

Intercessions: We pray this day
—for all those who labor in Christ's name.
—for all efforts at realizing the unity of Christ's one church.

WEEK IV—Thursday

Reconciliation with God

Opening Prayer: Loving God, whose essence is righteousness, we praise your name! We give thanks for this day and all it brings. Empower us to spend it as you have taught—keeping the faith, feeding the hungry, seeking justice for the oppressed, raising up those who are bowed down, and welcoming the stranger in our midst. By your power and our love of you, may we be known as those who are faithful in love, of the same mind as Christ. We pray that you will find in us those things that give you honor, even as this day honors you. Amen.

Reading from the Psalms   Psalm 146

Refrain: Happy are those whose hope is in the Lord their God.

Praise the LORD!
Praise the LORD, O my soul!
I will praise the LORD as long as I live;
    I will sing praises to my God all my life long.*

Do not put your trust in princes,
    in mortals, in whom there is no help.
When their breath departs, they return to the earth;
    on that very day their plans perish.

Happy are those whose help is the God of Jacob,
    whose hope is in the LORD their God,
who made heaven and earth,
    the sea, and all that is in them;

77

who keeps faith forever;
   who executes justice for the oppressed;
   who gives food to the hungry.*

The LORD sets the prisoners free;
   The LORD opens the eyes of the blind.
The LORD lifts up those who are bowed down;
   The LORD loves the righteous.
The LORD watches over the strangers;
   he upholds the orphan and the widow,
   but the way of the wicked he brings to ruin.*

The LORD will reign forever,
   your God, O Zion, for all generations.
Praise the LORD!

Reading from the New Testament   Philippians 2:1-13

   If then there is any encouragement in Christ, any consolation from love, any sharing in the Spirit, any compassion and sympathy, make my joy complete: be of the same mind, having the same love, being in full accord and of one mind. Do nothing from selfish ambition or conceit, but in humility regard others as better than yourselves. Let each of you look not to your own interests, but to the interests of others. Let the same mind be in you that was in Christ Jesus
   who, though he was in the form of God,
      did not regard equality with God
      as something to be exploited,
   but emptied himself,
      taking the form of a slave,
      being born in human likeness.
   And being found in human form,
      he humbled himself
      and became obedient to the point of death—
      even death on a cross.

   Therefore God also highly exalted him
      and gave him the name
      that is above every name,
   so that at the name of Jesus
      every knee should bend,
      in heaven and on earth and under the earth,
   and every tongue should confess

that Jesus Christ is Lord,
to the glory of God the Father.

Therefore, my beloved, just as you have always obeyed me, not only in my presence, but much more now in my absence, work out your own salvation with fear and trembling; for it is God who is at work in you, enabling you both to will and to work for his good pleasure.

Intercessions: We pray this day
—for God's presence in our decisions about lifestyle and priorities.
—for those for whom each day brings a search for food, shelter, and work.

WEEK IV—Friday

Reconciliation with Neighbor

Opening Prayer: God, we praise you for the beauty of the earth. Yet we confess that we take insufficient care of your creation. God, we thank you for the harvest you provide in abundance. Yet we confess that we distribute your gifts unevenly and that many of your children go hungry. God, we thank you for your promise of peace. Yet we confess that we are a warring people, killing our neighbors for selfish gain. God, we thank you for the revelation of your Son. Yet we confess that we are often blind to his presence among us. God, we thank you for the gift of faith. Yet we confess that our days are filled with doubt. Touch us! Heal us! Make us new! Amen.

Reading from the Psalms   Psalm 147:1-15, 19-20

Refrain: How good it is to sing praises to God.

Praise the LORD!
How good it is to sing praises to God;
    for he is gracious, and a song of praise is fitting.
The LORD builds up Jerusalem;
    he gathers the outcasts of Israel.

He heals the brokenhearted,
and binds up their wounds.
He determines the number of the stars;
he gives to all of them their names.
Great is our LORD, and abundant in power;
his understanding is beyond measure.
The LORD lifts up the downtrodden;
he casts the wicked to the ground.*

Sing to the LORD with thanksgiving;
make melody to our God on the lyre.
He covers the heavens with clouds,
prepares rain for the earth,
makes grass grow on the hills.
He gives to the animals their food,
and to the young ravens when they cry.
His delight is not in the strength of the horse,
nor his pleasure in the speed of a runner;
but the LORD takes pleasure in those who fear him,
in those who hope in his steadfast love.*

Praise the LORD, O Jerusalem!
Praise your God, O Zion!
For he strengthens the bars of your gates;
he blesses your children within you.
He grants peace within your borders;
he fills you with the finest of wheat.
He sends out his command to the earth;
his word runs swiftly.
He declares his word to Jacob,
his statutes and ordinances to Israel.
He has not dealt thus with any other nation;
they do not know his ordinances.
Praise the LORD!

Reading from the New Testament   Luke 4:16-30

When he came to Nazareth, where he had been brought up, he
went to the synagogue on the sabbath day, as was his custom. He
stood up to read, and the scroll of the prophet Isaiah was given to
him. He unrolled the scroll and found the place where it was
written:
"The Spirit of the Lord is upon me,
because he has annointed me

to bring good news to the poor.
He has sent me to proclaim release to the captives
and recovery of sight to the blind,
    to let the oppressed go free,
to proclaim the year of the Lord's favor."
And he rolled up the scroll, gave it back to the attendant, and sat down. The eyes of all in the synagogue were fixed on him. Then he began to say to them, "Today this scripture has been fulfilled in your hearing." All spoke well of him and were amazed at the gracious words that came from his mouth. They said, "Is not this Joseph's son?" He said to them, "Doubtless you will quote to me this proverb, 'Doctor, cure yourself!' And you will say, 'Do here also in your hometown the things that we have heard you did at Capernaum.'" And he said, "Truly I tell you, no prophet is accepted in the prophet's hometown. But the truth is, there were many widows in Israel in the time of Elijah, where the heaven was shut up three years and six months, and there was a severe famine over all the land; yet Elijah was sent to none of them except to a widow at Zarephath in Sidon. There were also many lepers in Israel in the time of the prophet Elisha, and none of them was cleansed except Naaman the Syrian." When they heard this, all in the synagogue were filled with rage. They got up, drove him out of the town, and led him to the brow of the hill on which their town was built, so that they might hurl him off the cliff. But he passed through the midst of them and went on his way.

Intercessions: We pray this day
    —for the neighbor we ignore or abuse.
    —for those in our midst who are poor, captive, or oppressed.

WEEK IV—Saturday

Reconciliation Within the Church

Opening Prayer: Good Creator of all that is, there are times when prayer comes easily to our lips, when praise for you and your creation wells up in us until it flows forth of its own accord. But there are other moments when our souls feel dry, when we are desperately in need of you but lack the thoughts and words to express our need. Be with us in those moments. Hold us close. Build us, like living stones, into the house of faith, until our very lives proclaim that you are God and greatly to be praised. Amen.

Reading from the Psalms   Psalm 148

Refrain: Praise the Lord from the heavens; praise God in the heights!

Praise the LORD!
Praise the LORD from the heavens;
    praise him in the heights!
Praise him, all his angels;
    praise him, all his host!

Praise him, sun and moon;
    praise him, all you shining stars!
Praise him, you highest heavens,
    and you waters above the heavens!

Let them praise the name of the LORD,
    for he commanded and they were created.
He established them forever and ever;
    he fixed their bounds, which cannot be passed.*

Praise the LORD from the earth,
    you sea monsters and all deeps,
fire and hail, snow and frost,
    stormy wind fulfilling his command!

Mountains and all hills,
    fruit trees and all cedars!
Wild animals and all cattle,
    creeping things and flying birds!

Kings of the earth and all peoples,
    princes and all rulers of the earth!
Young men and women alike,
    old and young together!*

Let them praise the name of the LORD,
    for his name alone is exalted;
    his glory is above earth and heaven.
He has raised up a horn for his people,
    praise for all his faithful,

for the people of Israel who are close to him.
Praise the LORD!

Reading from the New Testament   1 Peter 2:1-10

Rid yourselves, therefore, of all malice, and all guile, insincerity, envy, and all slander. Like newborn infants, long for the pure, spiritual milk, so that by it you may grow into salvation—if indeed you have tasted that the Lord is good.

Come to him, a living stone, though rejected by mortals yet chosen and precious in God's sight, and like living stones, let yourselves be built into a spiritual house, to be a holy priesthood, to offer spiritual sacrifices acceptable to God though Jesus Christ. For it stands in scripture:
"See, I am laying in Zion a stone,
a cornerstone chosen and precious;
and whoever believes in him will not be put to
shame."
To you then who believe, he is precious; but for those who do not believe,
"The stone that the builders rejected
has become the very head of the corner,"
and
"A stone that makes them stumble,
and a rock that makes them fall."
They stumble because they disobey the word, as they were destined to do.

But you are a chosen race, a royal priesthood, a holy nation, God's own people, in order that you may proclaim the mighty acts of him who called you out of darkness into his marvelous light.
Once you were not a people,
but now you are God's people;
once you had not received mercy,
but now you have received mercy.

Intercessions: We pray this day
—for the growth of God's church and its message of unity.
—for the work of ecumenical organizations and their efforts to end discord among Christians.

WEEK IV—Sunday

The Lord's Supper

Opening Prayer: Praise should be on our lips, O God, for with the dawn we see the glory of your creation once again. The signs of renewal are everywhere, yet we continue to live as if we were without hope. Why do we choose this road, O Lord, when you have promised to walk with us on a better road? Stir us up! You who remember not our sins, help us to cast off our deadening ways. Help us to turn from weeping to rejoicing. Remove the scales from our mind's eye that we might know you, the One who protects, instructs, and loves us. We ask these things through our Lord, Jesus Christ. Amen.

Reading from the Prophets   Isaiah 65:17-25

For I am about to create new heavens
    and a new earth;
the former things shall not be remembered
    or come to mind.
But be glad and rejoice forever
    in what I am creating;
for I am about to create Jerusalem as a joy,
    and its people as a delight.
I will rejoice in Jerusalem,
    and delight in my people;
no more shall the sound of weeping be heard in it,
    or the cry of distress.
No more shall there be in it
    an infant that lives but a few days,
    or an old person who does not live out a lifetime;
for one who dies at a hundred years will be considered a
        youth,
    and one who falls short of a hundred will be
        considered accursed
They shall build houses and inhabit them;
    they shall plant vineyards and eat their fruit.
They shall not build and another inhabit;
    they shall not plant and another eat;
for like the days of a tree shall the days of my people be,

and my chosen shall long enjoy the work of their hands.
They shall not labor in vain,
or bear children for calamity;
for they shall be offspring blessed by the LORD—
and their descendants as well.
Before they call I will answer,
while they are yet speaking I will hear.
The wolf and the lamb shall feed together,
the lion shall eat straw like the ox;
but the serpent—its food shall be dust!
They shall not hurt or destroy
on all my holy mountain,
says the LORD.

Reading from the New Testament   Luke 24:13-20, 28-35

Now on that same day two of them were going to a village called Emmaus, about seven miles from Jerusalem, and talking with each other about all these things that had happened. While they were talking and discussing, Jesus himself came near and went with them, but their eyes were kept from recognizing him. And he said to them, "What are you discussing with each other while you walk along?" They stood still, looking sad. Then one of them, whose name was Cleopas, answered him, "Are you the only stranger in Jerusalem who does not know the things that have taken place there in these days?" He asked them, "What things?" They replied, "The things about Jesus of Nazareth, who was a prophet mighty in deed and word before God and all the people, and how our chief priests and leaders handed him over to be condemned to death and crucified him.

As they came near the village to which they were going, he walked ahead as if he were going on. But they urged him strongly, saying, "Stay with us, because it is almost evening and the day is now nearly over." So he went in to stay with them. When he was at the table with them, he took bread, blessed and broke it, and gave it to them. Then their eyes were opened, and they recognized him; and he vanished from their sight. They said to each other, "Were not our hearts burning within us while he was talking to us on the road, while he was opening the scriptures to us?" That same hour they got up and returned to Jerusalem; and they found the eleven and their companions gathered together. They were saying, "The Lord has risen indeed, and he has appeared to Simon!" Then they told what had happened on the road, and how he had been made known to them in the breaking of the bread.

Intercessions: We pray this day

—for all those who are denied access to the Lord's Table.
—that the peace, joy, and unity of God's holy realm may increasingly mark our broken and sinful world.

Rejoice always, pray without ceasing,
give thanks in all circumstances; for this is the will of God
in Christ Jesus for you
(1 Thessalonians 5:16-18).

They devoted themselves to the apostles' teaching and fel-
lowship, to the breaking of bread and the prayers
(Acts 2:42).

Chapter III

Materials for Enhancing the Regular Cycle of Prayers

1. Prayers from the Universal Church

Each Christian is heir to an incredible legacy of prayer from the church of all times and places. Our spiritual horizons are inevitably expanded by making our own the prayers of ancient Europe or contemporary Africa.

This section is but a sample of such resources. Collections of contemporary prayers are widely available. We have selected "classic" prayers that should work well either as an opening prayer in the daily service or as a closing prayer following the intercessions.

O Thou, from whom to be turned is to fall,
to whom to be turned is to rise,
and in whom to stand is to abide forever;
grant us in all our duties thy help,
in all our perplexities thy guidance,
in all our dangers thy protection,
and in all our sorrows thy peace;
through Jesus Christ our Lord. Amen.

St. Augustine

Remember, O Lord, thy whole church;
all who join with us in prayer, all our brothers and sisters,
who stand in need of thy grace and succor.
Pour out upon them the riches of thy mercy,

so that we with them, redeemed in soul and body,
and steadfast in faith,
may ever praise thy wonderful and holy name;
through Jesus Christ our Lord. Amen.

Early Greek Liturgy (adapted)

O Lord our God, grant us grace to desire thee with our whole heart,
that so desiring, we may seek and find thee; and so finding thee we
may love thee; and loving thee we may hate those sins from which
thou hast redeemed us; for the sake of Jesus Christ. Amen.

St. Anselm

Lord, make us instruments of your peace.
Where there is hatred, let us sow love;
where there is injury, pardon;
where there is discord, union;
where there is doubt, faith;
where there is despair, hope;
where there is darkness, light;
where there is sadness, joy.
Grant that we may not so much seek to be consoled, as to console;
to be understood as to understand;
to be loved as to love. Hear us as we pray, "Our Creator",
For it is in giving that we receive;
it is in pardoning that we are pardoned;
and it is in dying that we are born to eternal life. Amen.

St. Francis of Assisi

God, of your goodness give me yourself for you are sufficient for
me. I cannot properly ask anything less, to be worthy of you. If I
were to ask less, I should always be in want. In you alone do I have
all. Amen.

Julian of Norwich

Teach us, good Lord,
to serve thee as thou deservest;
to give and not to count the cost;
to fight and not to heed the wounds;
to toil and not to seek for rest;
to labor and not to ask for any reward,

save that of knowing that we do thy will;
through Jesus Christ our Lord. Amen.

St. Ignatius Loyola

We would begin this day in devout meditations, in joy un-
speakable, and in blessing and praising thee, who hast given us
such good hope and everlasting consolation. Lift up our minds
above all these little things below, which are apt to distract our
thoughts; and keep them above till our hearts are fully bent to seek
thee every day in the way wherein Jesus hath gone before us.
Amen.

John Wesley[9]

We praise thee, O Lord, and unto thee we give thanks, for thy
merciful kindness is great toward us and thy faithfulness, O Lord,
endures forever. Save us, we beseech thee, from being so steeped
in care, so darkened by passion, or so thoughtless of thy presence,
that we pass unseeing and unheeding, even when the bush by the
wayside is aflame with thy glory. Open the eyes of our minds to the
tokens of thy power and goodness around and within us. And fill
our hearts, O Lord, with thy love, our mouths with thy praise, and
our lives with thy obedience, to the glory of thy name. Amen.

Walter Rauschenbusch[10]

God, give us grace to accept with serenity the things that cannot be
changed, courage to change the things that should be changed, and
the wisdom to distinguish the one from the other. Amen.

Reinhold Niebuhr[11]

O Lord, who has taught us that to gain the whole world and to lose
our souls is great folly, grant us the grace so to lose ourselves that
we may truly find ourselves anew in the life of grace, and so to
forget ourselves that we may be remembered in your kingdom.
Amen.

Reinhold Niebuhr[12]

O Lord, thou knowest all things; thou knowest that we love
thee. But thou also knowest that our hearts are divided among
several masters. Thou knowest our cowardice and how often we
have denied thee. Forgive us, Lord, and grant that this day we may

give ourselves to thee anew, humbly, resolutely, with a whole-hearted love. Amen.

Suzanne de Dietrich[13]

Thou who art over us, Thou who art one of us, Thou who art—also within us, may all see thee—in me also, may I prepare the way for thee, may I thank thee for all that shall fall to my lot, may I also not forget the needs of others, keep me in thy love as thou wouldest that all should be kept in mine. May everything in this my being be directed to thy glory and may I never despair. For I am under thy hand, and in thee is all power and goodness. Give me a pure heart—that I may see thee, a humble heart—that I may hear thee, a heart of love—that I may serve thee, a heart of faith—that I may abide in thee.

Dag Hammarskjöld[14]

Make us worthy, Lord, to serve our [neighbors] throughout the world who live and die in poverty or hunger. Give them, through our hands this day their daily bread, and by our understanding love, give peace and joy. Amen.

Mother Teresa[15]

Lord, we thank you that our churches are like big families.
Lord, let your spirit of reconciliation blow over all the earth.
    Let Christians live your love.
Lord, we praise you with Europe's cathedrals, with America's offerings,
    and with our African songs of praise.
Lord, we thank you that we have brothers [and sisters] in all the world. Be with them that make peace. Amen.

Fritz Pawelzik, ed.
I Sing Your Praise All the Day Long[16] (Africa)

O Lord, our heavenly Father,
You hear us praying here in Takoradi.
You hear our brothers [and sisters] praying in Africa,
in Asia, in Australia,
in America, and in Europe.
We are all one in prayer.

We praise and honor you,
and we beg you
that we may rightly carry out your commission:
to witness and to love,
in our church and throughout the whole world.
Accept our prayers graciously,
even when they are somewhat strange.
We praise you and pray to you
through Jesus Christ, our Lord.
Amen.

Fritz Pawelzik, ed.
I Lie on My Mat and Pray[17] (Africa)

2. Biblical Resources for Daily Prayer

A. "Invitatories": Opening Psalms

Several psalms have traditionally been used to begin the daily office (i.e., before the "opening prayer"). We commend the following for that purpose:

O come, let us sing to the LORD;
   let us make a joyful noise to the rock of our
      salvation!
Let us come into his presence with thanksgiving;
   let us make a joyful noise to him with songs of
      praise!
For the LORD is a great God,
   and a great King above all gods.
In his hand are the depths of the earth;
   the heights of the mountains are his also.
The sea is his, for he made it,
   and the dry land, which his hands have formed.

O come, let us worship and bow down,
   let us kneel before the LORD, our Maker!
For he is our God,
   and we are the people of his pasture,
   and the sheep of his hand.

Psalm 95:1-7

Make a joyful noise to the LORD, all the earth.
   Worship the LORD with gladness;
   come into his presence with singing.

Know that the LORD is God.
   It is he that made us, and we are his;
   we are his people, and the sheep of his pasture.

Enter his gates with thanksgiving,
   and his courts with praise.
   Give thanks to him, bless his name.

For the LORD is good;
   his steadfast love endures forever,
   and his faithfulness to all generations.
                                    Psalm 100

May God be gracious to us and bless us
   and make his face to shine upon us,
that your way may be known upon earth,
   your saving power among all nations.
Let the peoples praise you, O God;
   let all the peoples praise you.

Let the nations be glad and sing for joy,
   for you judge the peoples with equity
   and guide the nations upon earth.
Let the peoples praise you, O God;
   let all the peoples praise you.

The earth has yielded its increase;
   God our God, has blessed us.
May God continue to bless us;
   let all the ends of the earth revere him.
                                    Psalm 67

Praise the LORD!
Praise God in his sanctuary;
   praise him in his mighty firmament!
Praise him for his mighty deeds;
   praise him according to his surpassing greatness!

Praise him with trumpet sound;
  praise him with lute and harp!
Praise him with tambourine and dance;
  praise him with strings and pipe!
Praise him with clanging cymbals;
  praise him with loud clashing cymbals!
Let everything that breathes praise the Lord!
Praise the LORD!

Psalm 150

The earth is the LORD'S and all that is in it,
  the world, and those who live in it;
for he has founded it on the seas,
  and established it on the rivers.

Who shall ascend the hill of the LORD?
  And who shall stand in his holy place?
Those who have clean hands and pure hearts,
  who do not lift up their souls to what is false,
  and do not swear deceitfully.
They will receive blessings from the LORD,
  and vindication from the God of their salvation.
Such is the company of those who seek him,
  who seek the face of the God of Jacob.

Lift up your heads, O gates!
  and be lifted up, O ancient doors!
  that the King of glory may come in.

Who is the King of Glory?
  The LORD, strong and mighty,
  the LORD, mighty in battle.
Lift up your heads, O gates!
  and be lifted up, O ancient doors!
  that the King of glory may come in.
Who is this King of glory?
  The LORD of hosts,
  he is the King of glory.

Psalm 24

B. "Canticles": "Little Songs" from Scripture

The term *canticle* comes from the Latin *canticulum* ("little song") and refers to certain "songs" or poetic passages from biblical books other than the Psalms. They have long been part of the church's daily office and may appropriately be said or sung before or after the readings.

The three canticles most used in Christian worship are the following from the Gospel according to Luke:

The Song of Mary (Magnificat)

And Mary said,
"My soul magnifies the Lord,
  and my spirit rejoices in God my Savior,
for he has looked with favor on the lowliness of
             his servant.
      Surely, from now on all generations will call me
         blessed;
for the Mighty One has done great things for me,
  and holy is his name.
His mercy is for those who fear him
  from generation to generation.
He has shown strength with his arm;
  He has scattered the proud in the thoughts of
    their hearts.
He has brought down the powerful from their
    thrones,
  and lifted up the lowly;
he has filled the hungry with good things,
  and sent the rich away empty.
He has helped his servant Israel,
  in remembrance of his mercy,
according to the promise he made to our
    ancestors,
  to Abraham and to his descendants forever.
Luke 1:46-55

The Song of Zachariah (Benedictus Dominus Deus)

Blessed be the Lord God of Israel,
  for he has looked favorably on his people and
    redeemed them.
He has raised up a mighty savior for us
  in the house of his servant David,
as he spoke through the mouth of his holy
    prophets from of old,
  that we would be saved from our enemies and
    from the hand of all who hate us.
Thus he has shown the mercy promised to our
    ancestors,
  and has remembered his holy covenant,
the oath that he swore to our ancestor Abraham,
  to grant us that we, being rescued from the hands of
    our enemies,
might serve him without fear, in holiness and
    righteousness
  before him all our days.
And you, child, will be called the prophet of the Most
    High;
  for you will go before the Lord to prepare his ways,
to give knowledge of salvation to his people
  by the forgiveness of their sins.
By the tender mercy of our God,
  the dawn from on high will break upon us,
to give light to those who sit in darkness and in
  the shadow of death,
    to guide our feet into the way of peace."

Luke 1:68-79

The Song of Simeon (Nunc dimittis)

"Master, now you are dismissing your servant in
  peace, according to your word;
for my eyes have seen your salvation,
  which you have prepared in the presence of all
    peoples,
a light for revelation to the Gentiles
  and for glory to your people Israel."

Luke 2:29-32

Several passages from the Old Testament also fit nicely into a pattern of daily prayer and readings. See, for example, the two Songs of Moses (Exodus 15:1-18; Deuteronomy 32:1-43), the Song of Hannah (1 Samuel 2:1-10), the Song of Isaiah (Isaiah 12), the Song of Hezekiah (Isaiah 38:10-20), and the Song of Habakkuk (Habakkuk 3:2-19).

3. Alternative Forms for Intercessory Prayer

The four-week cycle of readings and prayers suggested in this book recommends no particular form for the prayers of intercession. We suspect that most members of "non-liturgical" traditions will feel comfortable offering these prayers spontaneously or having one leader speak them without much liturgical structure; but various alternatives are possible. In the following examples, the whole community—whether it be a single person or an entire congregation—would join in the italicized responses.

Example 1

With all our heart and with all our mind, let us pray to the Lord, saying, "Lord, have mercy."
For the peace of the world; especially for peace in _____, and for all those who work for reconciliation, let us pray to the Lord.

Lord, have mercy.

For the unity of the church, especially the church in _____, and for the strength to live as a reconciled people in this place, let us pray to the Lord.

Lord, have mercy.

For those who this day suffer need, illness, anxiety, or grief, and especially for _____, let us pray to the Lord.

Lord, have mercy.

Example 2

I ask your prayers for the church throughout the world (and especially in _____) that it may show forth faithful witness to the reconciling power of God. Let us pray for the church.

(Silent prayer)

I ask your prayers for those who this day are hungry and homeless that they may not be forgotten. Let us pray for those in need.

(Silent prayer)

I ask your prayers for the members of this community that we may learn to love God and neighbor more truly. Let us pray for ourselves.

(Silent prayer)

Example 3

God of universal love, we pray this day for those who suffer oppression because of race, religion, or place of origin. Strengthen us to call such sin by name and to work for its elimination. God, in your mercy,

Hear our prayer.

God of gracious creation, we pray this day for the earth you have made and called good. Guide us in the use of its resources that we may be stewards of your precious gifts. God, in your mercy,

Hear our prayer.

4. Seasonal Adaptations

The mystery of our salvation is so profound, the wonder of God's reconciling work in our lives is so rich, that no single theme or attitude can possibly comprehend it. That is why the church has historically divided the Christian year into seasons. During each season a particular aspect of the drama of redemption through Jesus Christ receives focused attention.

Season	Themes
Advent	Anticipation of Christ's birth and second coming; hope and preparation
Christmas	Incarnation; joyous response to God's self-giving
Epiphany	Manifestations of God in Christ; coming of the Magi; baptism of Jesus
Lent	Jesus' passion and the way of the cross; penitence, discipline, and confession; preparation for baptism
Easter	Resurrection of Jesus and his ascension; joy and hope
Pentecost	Coming of the Spirit; birth of the church and its continuing work and witness

Our daily prayer should reflect these changing emphases, especially during the pivotal seasons of Advent-Christmas and Lent-Easter. The following suggestions only scratch the surface of possible adaptations.

Lent. Many devotional booklets are available for the Lenten season. You might want to choose one and substitute its readings and meditations for the New Testament readings in our recommended cycle. Several psalms are particularly suited to the penitential character of Lent. Try beginning your time of prayer with Psalm 32,

51, or 130 in order to establish the attitude of confession. Finally, we recommend that the opening prayer reflect the season with its themes of passion, discipline, and confession. We offer two examples, the first a classic prayer of confession from the Anglican *Book of Common Prayer.*

Most merciful God,
we confess that we have sinned against you
in thought, word, and deed,
by what we have done,
and by what we have left undone.
We have not loved you with our whole heart;
we have not loved our neighbors as ourselves.
We are truly sorry and we humbly repent.
For the sake of your son Jesus Christ,
have mercy on us and forgive us;
that we may delight in your will,
and walk in your ways,
to the glory of your name. Amen.

Holy God, you have shown us in the passion of our Lord the way we should go, yet we confess that we so often follow a different road. Rather than glory in the cross of Jesus with its promise of new life, we glory in our own achievements and cling fast to the old. Forgive us, we pray. Renew in us the memory of our baptism when our sins were washed away. Fill us with a sure resolve to live no longer for ourselves but for him who died and rose for us. In his name we pray. Amen.

Advent. Since Advent is also a penitential season, the psalms suggested for Lent (especially Psalm 130) would be appropriate during these four weeks prior to Christmas. Such passages as Isaiah 40:3-5 or Psalm 62:1-7 might also be used as calls to worship in order to set the proper tone of hopeful expectation.

The biblical stories associated with Advent and Christmas provide a wealth of images for use in the opening prayer. The following are taken from the book *Thankful Praise: A Resource for Christian Worship.* [18]

101

Lord, you are coming
and we confess that we are not ready!
The place we provide for you is
less than the roughest manger.
The defenses we erect against you are
greater than those of the worried king.
By your loving presence in our lives, O God,
make smooth the rough places in our hearts.
Confound the defenses we have built.
Infect our wills with your goodness that we may
know Christ born anew in our midst and worship
    him.
Through Jesus Christ we pray. Amen.

God, we confess that ours is still a world
in which Herod seems to rule:
the powerful are revered,
the visions of the wise are ignored,
the poor are afflicted,
and the innocent are killed.
You show us that salvation comes
in the vulnerability of a child,
yet we hunger for the "security" of weapons and
    walls.
You teach us that freedom comes in loving service,
yet we trample on others in our efforts to be "free."
Forgive us, God, when we look to the palace
instead of the stable,
when we heed politicians more than prophets.
Renew us with the spirit of Bethlehem,
that we may be better prepared for your coming. Amen.

5. An Ecumenical Prayer Cycle

The Fifth Assembly of the World Council of Churches in
Nairobi (1975) recommended "that all churches should encourage
and assist their members in regular and informed intercession for
other churches" in order to strengthen the spiritual bonds among
Christians. Prayer of this sort anticipates the unity for which Christ

prayed (John 17:20-21) and which, Christians believe, is God's gift and intention. In response to this recommendation, the Council published an ecumenical prayer cycle, *For All God's People*, in 1978. The idea is simple and concrete: Each week throughout the year, the churches are invited to pray for the body of Christ in one particular part of the world. The material for each week provides a brief description of all the churches in the designated region or nation, suggestions for thanksgiving and intercession, and a prayer from that part of the world.

A new edition of the prayer cycle, entitled *With All God's People*, was published in 1989. The list that follows is taken from the new edition. Try adding this global perspective to your daily intercessions. Make an effort to learn about the country or countries for which you are praying in order that you may truly suffer when they suffer and rejoice when they rejoice (1 Corinthians 12:26).

Week 1: Egypt, Israel and the Occupied Territories, Jordan, Lebanon, Syria
Week 2: Countries of the Arabian Peninsula, Iran, Iraq
Week 3: Cyprus, Greece, Turkey
Week 4: Algeria, Libya, Morocco, Tunisia,
Week 5: Hong Kong, Macao, People's Republic of China, Taiwan
Week 6: Democratic People's Republic of Korea, Japan, Republic of Korea
Week 7: The Philippines
Week 8: Brunei, Malaysia, Singapore
Week 9: Denmark, Finland, Iceland, Norway, Sweden
Week 10: Republic of Ireland, United Kingdom
Week 11: Belgium, Luxembourg, The Netherlands
Week 12: France, Portugal, Spain
Week 13: Djibouti, Ethiopia, Somalia
Week 14: Sudan, Uganda
Week 15: Kenya, Tanzania
Week 16: Madagascar, Malawi, Zambia
Week 17: Brazil
Week 18: Argentina, Paraguay, Uruguay
Week 19: Bolivia, Chile, Peru
Week 20: Czechoslovakia, Poland
Week 21: Albania, Bulgaria, Yugoslavia
Week 22: Hungary, Romania
Week 23: Mongolia, Union of Soviet Socialist Republics

Week 24: Liberia, Sierra Leone
Week 25: Cape Verde, Guinea, Guinea–Bissau, Senegal, The Gambia
Week 26: Benin, Ghana, Ivory Coast, Togo
Week 27: Nigeria
Week 28: Kampuchea, Laos, Vietnam
Week 29: Burma, Thailand
Week 30: Indonesia
Week 31: United States of America
Week 32: Canada
Week 33: Australia, New Zealand
Week 34: The Pacific Islands
Week 35: The Islands of the Indian Ocean
Week 36: The Caribbean Islands, French Guyana, Guyana, Surinam
Week 37: Belize, Guatemala, Honduras, Mexico
Week 38: Costa Rica, El Salvador, Nicaragua, Panama
Week 39: Colombia, Ecuador, Venezuela
Week 40: Burkina Faso, Chad, Mali, Mauritania, Niger
Week 41: Cameroon, Central African Republic
Week 42: Congo, Equatorial Guinea, Gabon, Sao Tome and Principe
Week 43: Burundi, Rwanda, Zaire
Week 44: Federal Republic of Germany, German Democratic Republic
Week 45: Austria, Liechtenstein, Switzerland
Week 46: Italy, Malta
Week 47: Bangladesh, Bhutan, Nepal
Week 48: Afghanistan, Pakistan
Week 49: India, Sri Lanka
Week 50: Angola, Mozambique
Week 51: Botswana, Zimbabwe
Week 52: Lesotho, South Africa, Swaziland

6. The Common Lectionary

A lectionary is a listing of passages from the Bible arranged for systematic reading. When a lectionary is used as part of daily prayer, those using it are exposed to the full range of texts and themes in the biblical tradition.

The four-week cycle of readings and prayers printed in this book is intended to help individuals and groups develop the discipline of regular prayer and scriptural study. We recommend, however, that once this discipline is established, a lectionary be used in place of our very selective readings.

The listing of readings that follows is called the Common Lectionary. It has been produced by an ecumenical group of worship scholars based on the lectionary developed by the Roman Catholic Church following its Second Vatican Council. The Common Lectionary provides four readings, including a psalm, for each Sunday in a three-year cycle. (Year A begins with the first Sunday in Advent in 1989 and runs through 1990. Year B begins with the first Sunday in Advent of 1990. Year C begins with the first Sunday in Advent of 1991—and so on.) We recommend that persons use all or some of the readings in their daily prayer during the week prior to the Sunday on which the texts may be read as part of Sunday worship. This has the added benefit of preparing persons for the community's corporate service of thankful praise.

Daily lectionaries—i.e., different lists of readings for each day of the year—are also available and are to be commended. For example, the *Book of Common Prayer* of the Episcopal Church includes a two-year cycle of daily readings with the psalms arranged in a seven-week pattern that recurs throughout the year.

This may sound complicated, but the lectionary on the following pages should become quickly familiar with regular use.

TABLE OF READINGS AND PSALMS

(Versification follows that of the Revised Standard Version)

	First Sunday of Advent	Second Sunday of Advent	Third Sunday of Advent	Fourth Sunday of Advent
A. Lesson 1	Isa 2:1-5 Ps 122	Isa 11:1-10 Ps 72:1-8	Isa 35:1-10 Ps 146:5-10	Isa 7:10-16 Ps 24
Lesson 2	Rom 13:11-14	Rom 15:4-13	James 5:7-10	Rom 1:1-7
Gospel	Matt 24:36-44	Matt 3:1-12	Matt 11:2-11	Matt 1:18-25
B. Lesson 1	Isa 63:16-64:8 Ps 80:1-7	Isa 40:1-11 Ps 85:8-13	Isa 61:1-4, 8-11 Luke 1:46b-55	2 Sam 7:8-16 Ps 89:1-4,19-24
Lesson 2	1 Cor 1:3-9	2 Peter 3:8-15a	1 Thess 5:16-24	Rom 16:25-27
Gospel	Mark 13:32-37	Mark 1:1-8	John 1:6-8, 19-28	Luke 1:26-38
C. Lesson 1	Jer 33:14-16 Ps 25:1-10	Baruch 5:1-9 or Mal 3:1-4 Ps 126	Zeph 3:14-20 Isa 12:2-6	Micah 5:2-5a (5:1-4a) Ps 80:1-7
Lesson 2	1 Thess 3:9-13	Phil 1:3-11	Phil 4:4-9	Heb 10:5-10
Gospel	Luke 21:25-36	Luke 3:1-6	Luke 3:7-18	Luke 1:39-55

	Christmas, First Proper (Christmas Eve/Day)[1]	Christmas Second Proper (Add'l Lessons for Christmas Day)	Christmas Third Proper (Add'l Lessons for Christmas Day)
A. Lesson 1	Isa 9:2-7	Isa 62:6-7, 10-12	Isa 52:7-10
	Ps 96	Ps 97	Ps 98
Lesson 2	Titus 2:11-14	Titus 3:4-7	Hebr 1:1-12
Gospel	Luke 2:1-20	Luke 2:8-20	John 1:1-14

[1] The readings from the second and third propers for Christmas may be used as alternatives for Christmas day. If the third proper is not used on Christmas day, it should be used at some service during the Christmas cycle because of the significance of John's prologue.

	First Sunday after Christmas[2]	January 1-Name of Jesus Solemnity of Mary, Mother of God	January 1 (when observed as New Year)	Second Sunday after Christmas[3]
A. Lesson 1	Isa 63:7-9	Num 6:22-27	Deut 8:1-10	Jer 31:7-14 or Ecclus 24:1-4, 12-16
	Ps 111	Ps 67	Ps 117	Ps 147:12-20
Lesson 2	Heb 2:10-18	Gal 4:4-7 or Phil 2:9-13	Rev 21:1-6a	Eph 1:3-6, 15-18
Gospel	Matt 2:13-15, 19-23	Luke 2:15-21	Matt 25:31-46	John 1:1-18
B. Lesson 1	Isa 61:10-62:3 Ps 111		Eccles 3:1-13 Ps 8	
Lesson 2	Gal 4:4-7		Col 2:1-7	
Gospel	Luke 2:22-40		Matt 9:14-17	
C. Lesson 1	1 Sam 2:18-20, 26 or Ecclus 3:3-7, 14-17 Ps 111		Isa 49:1-10 Ps 90:1-12	
Lesson 2	Col 3:12-17		Eph 3:1-10	
Gospel	Luke 2:41-52		Luke 14:16-24	

[2]or the readings for Epiphany   [3]or the readings for Epiphany if not otherwise used.

	Epiphany	Baptism of the Lord (1st Sun. after Epiphany)[4]	2nd Sunday after Epiphany	3rd Sunday after Epiphany	4th Sunday after Epiphany
A. Lesson 1	Isa 60:1-6 Ps 72:1-14	Isa 42:1-9 Ps 29	Isa 49:1-7 Ps 40:1-11	Isa 9:1-4 Ps 27:1-6	Micah 6:1-8 Ps 27:1-11
Lesson 2	Eph 3:1-12	Acts 10:34-43	1 Cor 1:1-9	1 Cor 1:10-17	1 Cor 1:18-31
Gospel	Matt 2:1-12	Matt 3:13-17	John 1:29-34	Matt 4:12-23	Matt 5:1-12
B. Lesson 1		Gen 1:1-5 Ps 29	1 Sam 3:1-10, (11-20) Ps 63:1-8	Jonah 3:1-5, 10 Ps 62:5-12	Deut 18:15-20 Ps 111
Lesson 2		Acts 19:1-7	1 Cor 6:12-20	1 Cor 7:29-31 (32-35)	1 Cor 8:1-13
Gospel		Mark 1:4-11	John 1:35-42	Mark 1:14-20	Mark 1:21-28
C. Lesson 1		Isa 61:1-4 Ps 29	Isa 62:1-5 Ps 36:5-10	Neh 8:1-4a, 5-6, 8-10 Ps 19:7-14	Jer 1:4-10 Ps 71:1-6
Lesson 2		Acts 8:14-17	1 Cor 12:1-11	1 Cor 12:12-30	1 Cor 13:1-13
Gospel		Luke 3:15-17, 21-22	John 2:1-11	Luke 4:14-21	Luke 4:21-30

[4]In Leap Years, the number of Sundays after Epiphany will be the same as if Easter Day were one day later.

	5th Sunday after Epiphany	6th Sunday after Epiphany (Proper 1)	7th Sunday after Epiphany (Proper 2)	8th Sunday after Epiphany (Proper 3)	Last Sunday after Epiphany Transfiguration
A. Lesson 1	Isa 58:3-9a Ps 112:4-9	Deut 30:15-20 or Ecclus 15:15-20 Ps 119:1-8	Isa 49:8-13 Ps 62:5-12	Lev 19:1-2, 9-18 Ps 119:33-40	Exod 24:12-18 Ps 2:6-11
Lesson 2	1 Cor 2:1-11	1 Cor 3:1-9	1 Cor 3:10-11, 16-23	1 Cor 4:1-5	2 Peter 1:16-21
Gospel	Matt 5:13-16	Matt 5:17-26	Matt 5:27-37	Matt 5:38-48	Matt 17:1-9
B. Lesson 1	Job 7:1-7 Ps 147:1-11	2 Kings 5:1-14 Ps 32	Isa 43:18-25 Ps 41	Hos 2:14-20 Ps 103:1-13	2 Kings 2:1-12a Ps 50:1-6
Lesson 2	1 Cor 9:16-23	1 Cor 9:24-27	2 Cor 1:18-22	2 Cor 3:1-6	2 Cor 4:3-6
Gospel	Mark 1:29-39	Mark 1:40-45	Mark 2:1-12	Mark 2:18-22	Mark 9:2-9
C. Lesson 1	Isa 6:1-8 (9-13) Ps 138	Jer 17:5-10 Ps 1	Gen 45:3-11, 15 Ps 37:1-11	Ecclus 27:4-7 or Isa 55:10-13 Ps 92:1-4, 12-15	Exod 34:29-35 Ps 99
Lesson 2	1 Cor 15:1-11	1 Cor 15:12-20	1 Cor 15:35-38, 42-50	1 Cor 15:51-58	2 Cor 3:12-4:2
Gospel	Luke 5:1-11	Luke 6:17-26	Luke 6:27-38	Luke 6:39-49	Luke 9:28-36

111

	Ash Wednesday	1st Sunday of Lent	2nd Sunday of Lent	3rd Sunday of Lent	4th Sunday of Lent
A. Lesson 1	Joel 2:1-2, 12-17a Ps 51:1-12	Gen 2:4b-9, 15-17, 25-3:7 Ps 130	Gen 12:1-4a (4b-8) Ps 33:18-22	Exod 17:3-7 Ps 95	1 Sam 16:1-3 Ps 23
Lesson 2	2 Cor 5:20b-6:2 (3-10)	Rom 5:12-19	Rom 4:1-5, (6-12), 13-17	Rom 5:1-11	Eph 5:8-14
Gospel	Matt 6:1-6, 16-21	Matt 4:1-11	John 3:1-17 or Matt 17:1-9	John 4:5-26 (27-42)	John 9:1-41
B. Lesson 1		Gen 9:8-17 Ps 25:1-10	Gen 17:1-10, 15-19 Ps 105:1-11	Exod 20:1-17 Ps 19:7-14	2 Chron 36:14-23 Ps 137:1-6
Lesson 2		1 Peter 3:18-22	Rom 4:16-25	1 Cor 1:22-25	Eph 2:4-10
Gospel		Mark 1:9-15	Mark 8:31-38 or Mark 9:1-9	John 2:13-22	John 3:14-21
C. Lesson 1		Deut 26:1-11 Ps 91:9-16	Gen 15:1-12, 17-18 Ps 127	Exod 3:1-15 Ps 103:1-13	Joshua 5:9-12 Ps 34:1-8
Lesson 2		Rom 10:8b-13	Phil 3:17-4:1	1 Cor 10:1-13	2 Cor 5:16-21
Gospel		Luke 4:1-13	Luke 13:31-35 or Luke 9:28-36	Luke 13:1-9	Luke 15:1-3, 11-32

	5th Sunday of Lent	Lent 6 when observed as Passion Sunday	Lent 6 observed as Palm Sunday[5]
A. Lesson 1	Ezek 37:1-14 Ps 116:1-9	Isa 50:4-9a Ps 31:9-16	Isa 50:4-9a Ps 118:19-29
Lesson 2	Rom 8:6-11	Phil 2:5-11	Phil 2:5-11
Gospel	John 11:(1-16), 17-45	Matt 26:14-27:66 or Matt 27:11-54	Matt 21:1-11
B. Lesson 1	Jer 31:31-34 Ps 51:10-17	Same as A Ps 31:9-16	Same as A Ps 118:19-29
Lesson 2	Heb 5:7-10	Same as A	Same as A
Gospel	John 12:20-33	Mark 14:1-15:47 or Mark 15:1-39	Mark 11:1-11 or John 12:12-16
C. Lesson 1	Isa 43:16-21 Ps 126	Same as A Ps 31:9-16	Same as A Ps 118:19-29
Lesson 2	Phil 3:8-14	Same as A	Same as A
Gospel	John 12:1-8	Luke 22:14-23:56 or Luke 23:1-49	Luke 19:28-40

[5]These readings are provided for the liturgy or procession of palms for churches which have not had the tradition of readings-and-procession and also for an early "said" service in the Episcopal tradition.

113

Holy Week

	Monday	Tuesday	Wednesday	Holy Thursday[7]	Good Friday
A. Lesson 1	Isa 42:1-9 Ps 36:5-10	Isa 49:1-7 Ps 71:1-12	Isa 50:4-9a Ps 70	Exod 12:1-4 Ps 116:12-19	Isa 52:13-53:12 Ps 22:1-18
Lesson 2	Heb 9:11-15	1 Cor 1:18-31	Heb 12:1-3	1 Cor 11:23-26	Heb 4:14-16, 5:7-9
Gospel	John 12:1-11	John 12:20-36	John 13:21-30	John 13:1-15	John 18:1-19:42 or John 19:17-30
B. Lesson 1				Exod 24:3-8 Ps 116:12-19	
Lesson 2				1 Cor 10:16-17	
Gospel				Mark 14:12-26	
C. Lesson 1				Jer 31:31-34 Ps 116:12-19	
Lesson 2				Heb 10:16-25	
Gospel				Luke 22:7-20	

[6]for those who want the feet washing every year, "A" readings are used each year.
[7]Psalm 116 is used at the Lord's Supper on Holy Thursday. Psalm 89:20-21, 24, 26 is used at the "chrism" service.

Easter Vigil[8]

Old Testament Readings and Psalms (A, B, C)

Genesis 1:1-2:2
  Psalm 33
Genesis 7:1-5, 11-18; 8:6-18; 9:8-13
  Psalm 46
Genesis 22:1-18
  Psalm 16
Exodus 14:10-15:1
Exodus 15:1-6, 11-13, 17-18
Isaiah 54:5-14
  Psalm 30
Isaiah 55:1-11
Isaiah 12:2-6
Baruch 3:9-15, 32-4:4
  Psalm 19

Ezekiel 36:24-28
  Psalm 42
Ezekiel 37:1-14
  Psalm 143
Zephaniah 3:14-20
  Psalm 98

Second Reading (A, B, C)

Romans 6:3-11
  Psalm 114

Gospel
  A. Matthew 28:1-10
  B. Mark 16:1-8
  C. Luke 24:1-12

[8]This selection of readings and psalms is provided for the Easter Vigil. A minimum of three readings from the Old Testament should be used, and this should always include Exodus 14.

	Easter[9]	2nd Sunday of Easter	3rd Sunday of Easter	4th Sunday of Easter	5th Sunday of Easter
A. Lesson 1	Acts 10:34-43 or Jer 31:1-6 Ps 118:14-24	Acts 2:14a, 22-32 Ps 16:5-11	Acts 2:14a, 36-41 Ps 116:12-19	Acts 2:42-47 Ps 23	Acts 7:55-60 Ps 31:1-8
Lesson 2	Col 3:1-4 or Acts 10:34-43	1 Peter 1:3-9	1 Peter 1:17-23	1 Peter 2:19-25	1 Peter 2:2-10
Gospel	John 20:1-18 or Matt 28:1-10	John 20:19-31	Luke 24:13-35	John 10:1-10	John 14:1-14
B. Lesson 1	Acts 10:34-43 or Isa 25:6-9 Ps 118:14-24	Acts 4:32-35 Ps 133	Acts 3:12-19 Ps 4	Acts 4:8-12 Ps 23	Acts 8:26-40 Ps 22:25-31
Lesson 2	1 Cor 15:1-11 or Acts 10:34-43	1 John 1:1-2:2	1 John 3:1-7	1 John 3:18-24	1 John 4:7-12
Gospel	John 20:1-18 or Mark 16:1-8	John 20:19-31	Luke 24:35-48	John 10:11-18	John 15:1-8

C.					
Lesson 1	Acts 10:34-43 or Isa 65:17-25 Ps 118:14-24	Acts 5:27-32 Ps 2	Acts 9:1-20 Ps 30:4-12	Acts 13:15-16, 26-33 Ps 23	Acts 14:8-18 Ps 145:3b-21
Lesson 2	1 Cor 15:19-26 or Acts 10:34-43	Rev 1:4-8	Rev 5:11-14	Rev 7:9-17	Rev 21:1-6
Gospel	John 20:1-18 or Luke 24:1-12	John 20:19-31	John 21:1-19 or John 21:15-19	John 10:22-30	John 13:31-35

[9] If the Old Testament passage is chosen, the Acts passage is used as the second reading to initiate the sequential reading of Acts during the fifty days of Easter.

Easter Evening[10]

A.	
Lesson 1	Acts 5:29-32 or Dan 12:1-3 Ps 150
Lesson 2	1 Cor 5:6-8 or Acts 5:29-32
Gospel	Luke 24:13-49

[10] If the first reading is from the Old Testament, the reading from Acts should be second.

	6th Sunday of Easter	Ascension[11]	7th Sunday of Easter	Pentecost[12]	Trinity Sunday
A. Lesson 1	Acts 17:22-31	Acts 1:1-11	Acts 1:6-14	Acts 2:1-21 or Isa 44:1-8	Deut 4:32-40
	Ps 66:8-20	Ps 47	Ps 68:1-10	Ps 104:24-34	Ps 33:1-12
Lesson 2	1 Peter 3:13-22	Eph 1:15-23	1 Peter 4:12-14; 5:6-11	1 Cor 12:3b-13 or Acts 2:1-21	2 Cor 13:5-14
Gospel	John 14:15-21	Luke 24:46-53 or Mark 16:9-16, 19-20	John 17:1-11	John 20:19-23 or John 7:37-39	Matt 28:16-20
B. Lesson 1	Acts 10:44-48		Acts 1:15-17, 21-26	Acts 2:1-21 or Ezek 37:1-14	Isa 6:1-8
	Ps 98	Ps 47	Ps 1	Ps 104:24-34	Ps 29
Lesson 2	1 John 5:1-6		1 John 5:9-13	Rom 8:22-27 or Acts 2:1-21	Rom 8:12-17
Gospel	John 15:9-17		John 17:11b-19	John 15:26-27; 16:4b-15	John 3:1-17

C. Lesson 1	Acts 15:1-2, 22-29 Ps 67	Ps 47	Acts 16:16-34 Ps 97	Acts 2:1-21 or Gen 11:1-9 Ps 104:24-34	Prov 8:22-31 Ps 8
Lesson 2	Rev 21:10, 22-27		Rev 22:12-14, 16-17, 20	Rom 8:14-17 or Acts 2:1-21	Rom 5:1-5
Gospel	John 14:23-29		John 17:20-26	John 14:8-17,	John 16:12-15 25-27

[11] Or on the Seventh Sunday of Easter.
[12] If the Old Testament passage is chosen for the first reading, the Acts passage is used as the second reading.

	Proper 4[13] Sunday between May 29 and June 4 inclusive (if after Trinity Sunday)	Proper 5 Sunday between June 5 and 11 inclusive (if after Trinity Sunday)	Proper 6 Sunday between June 12 and 18 inclusive (if after Trinity Sunday)	Proper 7 Sunday between June 19 and 25 inclusive (if after Trinity Sunday)	Proper 8 Sunday between June 26 and July 2 inclusive
A. Lesson 1	Gen 12:1-9 Ps 33:12-22	Gen 22:1-18 Ps 13	Gen 25:19-34 Ps 46	Gen 28:10-17 Ps 91:1-10	Gen 32:22-32 Ps 17:1-7, 15
Lesson 2	Rom 3:21-28	Rom 4:13-18	Rom 5:6-11	Rom 5:12-19	Rom 6:3-11
Gospel	Matt 7:21-29	Matt 9:9-13	Matt 9:35-10:8	Matt 10:24-33	Matt 10:34-42
B. Lesson 1	1 Sam 16:1-13 Ps 20	1 Sam 16:14-23 Ps 57	2 Sam 1:1, 17-27 Ps 46	2 Sam 5:1-12 Ps 48	2 Sam 6:1-15 Ps 24
Lesson 2	2 Cor 4:5-12	2 Cor 4:13-5:1	2 Cor 5:6-10, 14-17	2 Cor 5:18-6:2	2 Cor 8:7-15
Gospel	Mark 2:23-3:6	Mark 3:20-35	Mark 4:26-34	Mark 4:35-41	Mark 5:21-43
C. Lesson 1	1 Kgs 8:22-23, 41-43 Ps 100	1 Kgs 17:17-24 Ps 113	1 Kgs 19:1-8 Ps 42	1 Kgs 19:9-14 Ps 43	1 Kgs 19:15-21 Ps 44:1-8
Lesson 2	Gal 1:1-10	Gal 1:11-24	Gal 2:15-21	Gal 3:23-39	Gal 5:1,13-25
Gospel	Luke 7:1-10	Luke 7:11-17	Luke 7:36-8:3	Luke 9:18-24	Luke 9:51-62

[13]If the Sunday between May 24 and 28 inclusive follows Trinity Sunday, use Eighth Sunday after Epiphany on that day.

	Proper 9 Sunday between July 3 and 9 inclusive	Proper 10 Sunday between July 10 and 16 inclusive	Proper 11 Sunday between July 17 and 23 inclusive	Proper 12 Sunday between July 24 and 30 inclusive	Proper 13 Sunday between July 31 and Aug. 6 inclusive
A. Lesson 1	Exod 1:6-14, 22–2:10 Ps 124	Exod 2:11-22 Ps 69:6-15	Exod 3:1-12 Ps 103:1-13	Exod 3:13-20 Ps 105:1-11	Exod 12:1-14 Ps 143:1-10
Lesson 2	Rom 7:14-25a	Rom 8:9-17	Rom 8:18-25	Rom 8:26-30	Rom 8:31-39
Gospel	Matt 11:25-30	Matt 13:1-9, 18-23	Matt 13:24-30, 36-43	Matt 13:44-52	Matt 14:13-21
B. Lesson 1	2 Sam 7:1-17 Ps 89:20-37	2 Sam 7:18-29 Ps 132:11-18	2 Sam 11:1-15 Ps 53	2 Sam 12:1-14 Ps 32	2 Sam 12:15b-24 Ps 34:11-22
Lesson 2	2 Cor 12:1-10	Eph 1:1-10	Eph 2:11-22	Eph 3:14-21	Eph 4:1-6
Gospel	Mark 6:1-6	Mark 6:7-13	Mark 6:30-34	John 6:1-15	John 6:24-35
C. Lesson 1	1 Kgs 21:1-3, 17-21 Ps 5:1-8	2 Kgs 2:1,6-14 Ps 139:1-12	2 Kgs 4:8-17 Ps 139:13-18	2 Kgs 5:1-15ab ("...in Israel") Ps 21:1-7	2 Kgs 13:14-20a Ps 28
Lesson 2	Gal 6:7-18	Col 1:1-14	Col 1:21-29	Col 2:6-15	Col 3:1-11
Gospel	Luke 10:1-12, 17-20	Luke 10:25-37	Luke 10:38-42	Luke 11:1-13	Luke 12:13-21

	Proper 14 Sunday between Aug 7 and 13 inclusive	Proper 15 Sunday between Aug 14 and 20 inclusive	Proper 16 Sunday between Aug 21 and 27 inclusive	Proper 17 Sunday between Aug 28 and Sep 3 inclusive	Proper 18 Sunday between Sep 4 and 10 inclusive
A. Lesson 1	Exod 14:19-31 Ps 106:4-12	Exod 16:2-15 Ps 78:1-3, 10-20	Exod 17:1-7 Ps 95	Exod 19:1-9 Ps 114	Exod 19:16-24 Ps 115:1-11
Lesson 2	Rom 9:1-5	Rom 11:13-16, 29-32	Rom 11:33-36	Rom 12:1-13	Rom 13:1-10
Gospel	Matt 14:22-33	Matt 15:21-28	Matt 16:13-20	Matt 16:21-28	Matt 18:15-20
B. Lesson 1	1 Sam 18:1, 5, 9-15 Ps 143:1-8	2 Sam 18:24-33 Ps 102:1-12	2 Sam 23:1-7 Ps 67	1 Kgs 2:1-4, 10-12 Ps 121	Ecclus 5:8-15 or Prov 2:1-8 Ps 119:129-136
Lesson 2	Eph 4:25-5:2	Eph 5:15-20	Eph 5:21-33	Eph 6:10-20	James 1:17-27
Gospel	John 6:35, 41-51	John 6:51-58	John 6:55-69	Mark 7:1-8, 14-15, 21-23	Mark 7:31-37
C. Lesson 1	Jer 18:1-11 Ps 14	Jer 20:7-13 Ps 10:12-18	Jer 28:1-9 Ps 84	Ezek 18:1-9, 25-29 Ps 15	Ezek 33:1-11 Ps 94:12-22
Lesson 2	Heb 11:1-3, 8-19	Heb 12:1-2, 12-17	Heb 12:18-29	Heb 13:1-8	Philemon 1-20
Gospel	Luke 12:32-40	Luke 12:49-56	Luke 13:22-30	Luke 14:1,7-14	Luke 14:25-33

	Proper 19 Sunday between Sep 11 and 17 inclusive	Proper 20 Sunday between Sep 18 and 24 inclusive	Proper 21 Sunday between Sep 25 and Oct 1 inclusive	Proper 22 Sunday between Oct 2 and 8 inclusive	Proper 23 Sunday between Oct 9 and 15 inclusive
A. Lesson 1	Exod 20:1-20 Ps 19:7-14	Exod 32:1-14 Ps 106:7-8, 19-23	Exod 33:12-23 Ps 99	Num 27:12-23 Ps 81:1-10	Deut 34:1-12 Ps 135:1-14
Lesson 2	Rom 14:5-12	Phil 1:21-27	Phil 2:1-13	Phil 3:12-21	Phil 4:1-9
Gospel	Matt 18:21-35	Matt 20:1-16	Matt 21:28-32	Matt 21:33-43	Matt 22:1-14
B. Lesson 1	Prov 22:1-2, 8-9 Ps 125	Job 28:20-28 Ps 27:1-6	Job 42:1-6 Ps 27:7-14	Gen 2:18-24 Ps 128	Gen 3:8-19 Ps 90:1-12
Lesson 2	James 2:1-5, 8-10, 14-17	James 3:13-18	James 4:13-17, 5:7-11	Heb 1:1-4, 2:9-11	Heb 4:1-3, 9-13
Gospel	Mark 8:27-38	Mark 9:30-37	Mark 9:38-50	Mark 10:2-16	Mark 10:17-30
C. Lesson 1	Hos 4:1-3, 5:15-6:6 Ps 77:11-20	Hos 11:1-11 Ps 107:1-9	Joel 2:23-30 Ps 107:1, 33-43	Amos 5:6-7, 10-15 Ps 101	Micah 1:2;2:1-10 Ps 26
Lesson 2	1 Tim 1:12-17	1 Tim 2:1-7	1 Tim 6:6-19	2 Tim 1:1-14	2 Tim 2:8-15
Gospel	Luke 15:1-10	Luke 16:1-13	Luke 16:19-31	Luke 17:5-10	Luke 17:11-19

	Proper 24 Sunday between Oct 16 and 22 inclusive	Proper 25 Sunday between Oct 23 and 29 inclusive	Proper 26 Sunday between Oct 30 and Nov 5 inclusive	Proper 27 Sunday between Nov 6 and 12 inclusive	Proper 28 Sunday between Nov 13 and 19 inclusive
A. Lesson 1	Ruth 1:1-19a Ps 146	Ruth 2:1-13 Ps 128	Ruth 4:7-17 Ps 127	Amos 5:18-14 Ps 50:7-15	Zeph 1:7, 12-18 Ps 76
Lesson 2	1 Thess 1:1-10	1 Thess 2:1-8	1 Thess 2:9-13, 17-20	1 Thess 4:13-18	1 Thess 5:1-11
Gospel	Matt 22:15-22	Matt 22:34-46	Matt 23:1-12	Matt 25:1-13	Matt 25:14-30
B. Lesson 1	Isa 53:7-12 Ps 35:17-28	Jer 31:7-9 Ps 126	Deut 6:1-9 Ps 119:33-48	1 Kgs 17:8-16 Ps 146	Dan 7:9-14 Ps 145:8-13
Lesson 2	Heb 4:14-16	Heb 5:1-6	Heb 7:23-28	Heb 9:24-28	Heb 10:11-18
Gospel	Mark 10:35-45	Mark 10:46-52	Mark 12:28-34	Mark 12:38-44	Mark 13:24-32
C. Lesson 1	Hab 1:1-3, 2:1-4 Ps 119:137-144	Zeph 3:1-9 Ps 3	Hag 2:1-9 Ps 65:1-8	Zech 7:1-10 Ps 9:11-20	Mal 4:1-6 (3:19-24 in Heb.) Ps 82
Lesson 2	2 Tim 3:14-4:5	2 Tim 4:6-8, 16-18	2 Thess 1:5-12	2 Thess 2:13-3:5	2 Thess 3:6-13
Gospel	Luke 18:1-8	Luke 18:9-14	Luke 19:1-10	Luke 20:27-38	Luke 21:5-19

**Proper 29
(Christ the King)
Sunday between
Nov 20 and 26
inclusive**

A. Lesson 1   Ezek 34:11-16, 20-24
               Ps 23

   Lesson 2   1 Cor 15:20-28

   Gospel   Matt 25:31-46

B. Lesson 1   Jer 23:1-6
               Ps 93

   Lesson 2   Rev 1:4b-8

   Gospel   John 18:33-37

C. Lesson 1   2 Sam 5:1-5
               Ps 95

   Lesson 2   Col 1:11-20

   Gospel   John 12:9-19

	Annunciation March 25	Visitation May 31	Presentation February 2	Holy Cross September 14
A. Lesson 1	Isa 7:10-14 Ps 45 or 40:6-10	1 Sam 2:1-10 Ps 113	Mal 3:1-4 Ps 84 or 24:7-10	Num 21:4b-9 Ps 98:1-5 or 78:1-2,34-38
Lesson 2	Heb 10:4-10	Rom 12:9-16b	Heb 2:14-18	1 Cor 1:18-24
Gospel	Luke 1:26-38	Luke 1:39-57	Luke 2:22-40	John 3:13-17

	All Saints, November 1[14]	Thanksgiving Day[15]
A. Lesson 1	Rev 7:9-17 Ps 34:1-10	Deut 8:7-18 Ps 65
Lesson 2	1 John 3:1-3	2 Cor 9:6-15
Gospel	Matt 5:1-12	Luke 17:11-19
B. Lesson 1	Rev 21:1-6a Ps 24:1-6	Joel 2:21-27 Ps 126
Lesson 2	Col 1:9-14	1 Tim 2:1-7
Gospel	John 11:32-44	Matt 6:25-33
C. Lesson 1	Dan 7:1-3, 15-18 Ps 149	Deut 26:1-11 Ps 100
Lesson 2	Eph 1:11-23	Phil 4:4-9
Gospel	Luke 6:20-36	John 6:25-35

[14]or on first day in November.
[15]readings *ad libitum*, not tied to A, B, or C.

Notes

1. R.C.C. Jasper, ed., *The Daily Office.* S.P.C.K. and Epworth Press, 1968.
2. Quoted in Jasper, *The Daily Office.*
3. Quoted in Paul F. Bradshaw, *Daily Prayer in the Early Church* . Oxford University Press, 1982, pp. 65-66.
4. *Ibid.*, p. 111.
5. James F. White, *Introduction to Christian Worship.* Abing don Press, 1980, p. 119.
6. Bradshaw, *Daily Prayer in the Early Church,* pp. 150-154.
7. Quoted in Robert Taft, *The Liturgy of the Hours in East and West.* Liturgical Press, 1986, p. 353.
8. C.P.M. Jones, "Liturgy and Personal Devotion" in Cheslyn Jones, Geoffrey Wainwright and Edward Yarnold, eds. *The Study of Spirituality.* Oxford University Press, 1986, p. 6.
9. Frederick C. Gill, ed., *John Wesley's Prayers.* Abingdon-Cokesbury Press, 1951, p. 60.
10. Walter Rauschenbusch, *Prayers of the Social Awakening.* Pilgrim Press, 1910.
11. George Appleton, ed., *Oxford Book of Prayer.* Oxford University Press, 1985, p. 60.
12. *Ibid.*, p. 119.
13. Venite Adoremus II (WSCF) no date given.
14. Appleton, *Oxford Book of Prayer,* pp. 84-85.
15. *Ibid.*, pp. 75-76.
16. Friendship Press, 1967.
17. Friendship Press, 1964.
18. *Thankful Praise.* CBP Press, 1987, pp. 67 and 68.